Praise for Naked in the River

As Khamsaly continues to circle back to tender moments with her sister and the impact that her death had on her and her family, she holds a magnifying glass to the long-lasting effects of sibling relationships. [Naked in the River] is a heartfelt...collection of musings on love, family, growth, and loss.

—Kirkus Reviews

Khamsaly's memoir takes you on a journey. It's raw, humble, sad and funny. There were chapters that caused me to tear up and quite a few that had me laughing out loud. A good read. It's beautiful.

—Ruah Wray
Author of *When Water Caught Fyre*

Khamsaly is a brilliant writer! Bravo! Can't put it down.

—Renee Martin
Singer-songwriter, producer
Background vocalist: Faith Hill/Tim McGraw

Loving how vulnerable this book is.

—Sadie Fagan, *Trinity County Superwoman*

I appreciate how much courage, honesty, faith, love and humor Khamsaly puts into her book! Beautiful, brave work.

—Peter Jain
Author of *Let the Dance Begin: Greetings from Humboldt*

Heartfelt and honest. I couldn't put it down.

—Ranee Kletchka
Educator/jewelry designer

If you love a great autobiography, this book's for you. Loved it.

—Jim Quinton
Music promoter/radio personality: *Jim's Mountain Country*

NAKED IN THE RIVER

NAKED IN THE RIVER

ARIANNA V. KHAMSALY

BLACKBERRY MOONSHINE PRESS

2022

Published by Blackberry Moonshine Press

ISBN: 978-0-578-33726-5

Cover photo of the author by Chloë Jade Reiter

Book design and production by Lucky Valley Press
Jacksonville Oregon www.luckyvalleypress.com

Printed on acid-free paper.

This memoir is an honest recollection of actual events in the author's life. The situations, places, and conversations have been recreated from memory. The names and identifying details of certain individuals have been changed to protect their privacy.

Contents

Introduction

My name is Arianna. I like tofu, short walks on the beach and being the first to laugh at my own jokes. Hell, sometimes the only one to laugh.

My life lies somewhere between debilitating grief and immaculate joy. Always striving for the joy end of the spectrum, often failing to reach it.

I am a secretary by day and a singer-songwriter by night. I prefer my night job. It's the only one that feeds my soul.

Sometimes at my desk during work hours this overwhelming emotion washes over me. A type of desperation that I can't accurately describe; this feeling that hurts. Painful deep sharpness inside my chest. No, not heart attack symptoms. My heart is fine. Physically fine, anyway.

But hearts are funny things. The only way I know how to exist is by following mine, yet it hasn't always led me in the right direction.

Even the misadventures have been interesting, though. Let me tell you all about it. The good and the bad. And everything between the lines.

I'm glad you're here.

Chapter 1

Bullshit

"Sounds like bullshit to me."

Tears stung my face and I felt like I was having an out of body experience as I heard the words spill from his mouth. His voice sounded distant, biting and aggressive simultaneously. I'd been crying all day as I worked on a note explaining why I could not stay married to him. I poured my heart out on that piece of paper. Told him how sorry I was multiple times. Even lied and said it wasn't his fault.

He met my words with, "Sounds like bullshit to me."

Looking back, I guess I'm glad that was how my ex-husband chose to deal with me divorcing him. I've always thought that if he loved me like he said he did, he would have asked me to stay. He would have said or done anything to try to make me believe he could change. All that would have done is draw out one of the worst moments of both of our lives. I'm glad he met my soulful apology and goodbye note with nothing but a smart-ass remark. It made it easier.

As time went on, our girls told me how sad he was that I left him. They indicated that he was crushed and that he wanted to spend the rest of his life with me. This was odd, because he hadn't seemed even remotely in love with me anymore. But then again, he always expressed his emotions, or lack thereof, in unusual ways. If I brought up a tough conversation, he would crack a joke. I would beg him to stop drinking too much, he tuned me out. He found stupid reasons to get mad so he could leave me alone all night in strange hotel rooms on road trips. I only realized years afterwards that he was probably out sleeping with other women or doing drugs while I waited, scared and alone, wondering if he was ever coming back. His default behaviors and deflections became tiresome. This was never a marriage based on equality or fairness. It was based on the fact that I unexpectedly got pregnant at nineteen years old and his well meaning family insisted that the entire world would explode if we did not legally wed before the baby was born. So I found myself standing in the local courthouse with a blue velvet dress covering my three months pregnant belly. Saying "I do" to a man who gave me a second child two and a half years after the first, and a whole lot of memories. Some I wish I could forget.

Don't get me wrong, I did love him. I am not writing this to claim he had no good qualities. He was brilliant. Always at the top of his class. I admired that about him. He had an intensity that drew me in. To this day I wish him well. I give him credit for always letting our daughters know how much he loves them. He put them through a lot of things that would break most parent/child bonds, but our girls still love him and feel his love. I commend him for that.

When we were first together I loved him fiercely, but I was blind to all the red flags. I thought they were just pretty house decorations. Useful for wiping down counter tops. I thought his huge pot consumption was a phase. I assumed it was normal to throw up and morph into a different person every time he drank. He was cold and frequently arrogant. The young heart can forgive so much. But only for so long...

During our marriage Jason often behaved as if he were the only one in it. He made major decisions without running a single detail by me. It was as if it was his life and his alone, and I was a minor aspect in it. Meant to be swept off to the side most of the time, except when he wanted something from me. He would take one of our daughters to get her ears pierced on a whim without bothering to let me know. And I remember on one particular day arriving home to see that he had turned a large swath of the field behind our house into a pen for two goats that, for some unknown reason, he purchased on his way back from town. Huge goats. I love animals, but I wasn't too sure about this idea. One of them was aggressive and tried to head-butt the girls with her hard skull and sharp horns. I missed our beautiful open field. It was one of my favorite things about our property. I liked to look out the window and see that open space. Peaceful and expansive, filled with wild flowers in springtime.

I think the reason I was so bothered by my ex-husband's behavior was that it made me feel powerless over my own life; like I could *have* an opinion, but it wasn't going to change anything, because he would do what he would do whether I liked it or not. It was difficult being a young mom and not feeling like I had a safe, stable male figure around. I was reluctant to ask for help with disciplining the kids because he could be so harsh with his tactics. I'm sure some of our differences were simple male/female aspects in origin. But there was more to it than that.

As the years wore on, I became more and more unhappy. I grew tired of seeing Jason's erratic behavior in public and exhausted with wondering what type of drugs or alcohol he had over consumed when I found him in an agitated or comatose state. I could only handle so many times of rushing to town to put an emergency "class canceled" sign on the door of his martial arts dojo before getting sick of covering for his odd behavior and addictions. I felt like I had too many family secrets to keep track of. Too much to hide. While he was busy becoming a black belt in kenpo karate, I was busy becoming a master at compensating for his dysfunctions. And presenting an outward persona like we were the perfect couple and I was a happy wife.

It got to the point where all I had to do was smell a hint of alcohol on his breath and I would feel sick. Full of angry despair. Substances controlled our lives, and I worried about the girls' safety when they were with their father. How could he respond appropriately if the kids got hurt and needed him when he was in a drunken stupor?

Because of all my years spent with an addict who had emotional health issues, I'm afraid I adopted a rather intolerant view of alcoholism and drug abuse. They say it's a disease, and I try hard to understand, but when it burns down your whole life as you know it, it becomes harder to see it as a disease, and easier to see it as someone choosing to be uncaring, destructive, and selfish. I was never lonelier than during my years with Jason. My soul became desolate. I tried to stop wanting things from him and in doing so I continually denied my own feelings and emotional needs. This was a dangerous combination, because I found myself having strong attractions to other men. Men who seemed warm, open hearted, and caring. I beat myself up every time this happened, and I told myself it was normal. But it wasn't normal. Yes, we notice here and there a person attractive to our eye. *That* is normal. But my intense struggling was a symptom that something was dreadfully wrong in my marriage and in my life.

I resolved to remedy the problem by leaving my marriage at the age of twenty-nine. I met him when I was barely eighteen, gave him almost my entire twenties, and had many regrets I failed to fully understand until that point in time. I didn't realize what I gave up while trying to be a "good girl" and stay entrenched in my marital status. I don't think anyone gets married thinking they will get divorced. Most human beings are well meaning, dedicated to doing the right thing. Women tend to sacrifice their own happiness for the sake of their children and partners. Tragically, we do this often. But I was done sacrificing. It was time for me to stop giving myself the short end of the deal and pretending it was okay. I was ready to make a run for it. I was ready to *live*.

Chapter 2

Aftermath

Like so many women who leave a bad marriage, I didn't take enough with me. I left almost everything I owned in the house I shared with Jason. Soul-crushing guilt over leaving him burned through me like a fever, but I knew it was the only right thing to do. Clothes and jewelry, a few picture albums, my kids every other week. Those were the belongings I took. Over the years I've often thought about an item I liked and wondered where I stored it, only to realize, as if for the first time, that I left it behind in my past life. There are still a few things I look for now and then, because I sincerely don't know whether I have them in my possession or not. A pretty little vase we had purchased at a Saturday market in Eugene, Oregon. An Olson's Stoneware serving dish I loved. I assume I left them sitting on the shelf as I drove away from our house for the last time. Never looking back except to make sure my past wasn't following me too closely.

I didn't start out my new life as a single mother in any sort of glamourous fashion. Quite the contrary, really. Moving in with my father, I had a tiny but cute little room the girls and I shared. I'll never forget the deep loneliness during the first week they spent with their dad. Lying down on my futon, I'd try to read a book so my mind would stop focusing on how much I missed my children. My heart ached and I felt like a terrible parent for putting them through such trauma. My daughters were still young. Such cuties. My little peanuts. I felt like a kid myself when separated from them. Realizing how much I was accustomed to their daily noises and chatter. The tiny spare room I was living in, while trying to figure out how to live on my own, felt eerily quiet. Too quiet. As if no life hung in the air. Only empty space and microscopic particles of dust that began to settle on my soul.

It was strange to be single for the first time in my adult life. Equal parts thrilling and terrifying. With an aspect of insecurity thrown into the mix. What the heck would it be like to be thrust into the dating scene? Dating? What was that? I hadn't really even dated Jason. I mean, we got to know each other at first, but not over meals or drinks at restaurants.

Rather, we ran into each other a couple times at gatherings, then started hanging out at his mom's place. For some reason we just "were" without the standard lead-up of most relationships.

So here I was, almost thirty years old, only having slept with the father of my children, anticipating my first date someday down the road. And more pressingly, anticipating what the heck I was going to do with my life now that it was my own. How would I support myself? Was I going to live in this little room at my dad's forever? Was I going to be *that adult child he can never seem to push from the nest?* I hoped not. I appreciated him taking me under his wing at a time when I needed his help more than ever, but I didn't want to get too comfortable. I needed to make sure I kept the fire under me burning bright and burning hot. So I would make headway fast and learn to be self-sufficient.

But, becoming self-sufficient proved to be harder than I expected. And it didn't help that Jason had unilaterally cancelled our joint credit card. I've wondered many times why that was legal. Shouldn't the company have consulted me first? It caused mayhem with my credit for a long time and bills in collections because I had no way to pay medical or dental dues in full.

I lived in that little room at my father's house for six months. Long enough to find a new job and a home to rent for me and my girls. As luck would have it, that home was located directly across the street from my dad's. I walked the few things I owned right across the road and into my rental. A large, strange brick building that looked like a fortress. The masonry was drab greyish tan and the inside was like a time capsule from the nineteen-seventies.

Once the girls and I officially settled into our new home, I found it doubly hard when they were away. Those weeklong stints felt like an eternity. All I wanted was to have them home. Looking back now I wish I had pushed for full custody from the start, with visitation rights and maybe weekends with their father. They went through so many unnecessarily harrowing experiences with him during his custodial weeks. Not because he was purposefully harming them, but because his life was turned upside down in so many ways that he could not provide stability. I tried to be amicable and share our kids equally, but the girls were caught in the middle. And they weren't getting what they needed when they were away from me. Too often they saw him drunk beyond coherency or on manic highs from hard drugs. A lot of the worst stories the girls only shared with me years later, after they were solely in my care. Not as a way to bash their father, but to express the trauma and work through it. I wish I could go back in time and erase what they went through. I hope they know that when they were away from me all those weeks all I could think about was the very second they would walk back through my door with excited smiles on their faces.

The first night I got them back was always a celebration. We had so much to catch up on. So many hugs to stockpile. We loved watching movies and playing ping-pong in the back room. On the table that a girlfriend lent me, when she saw what an oddly big, empty back room I had. We perched at windows, looking at foxes. The sweet creatures loved to eat the fallen cherries from the tree in our yard. Our girl time was invaluable to me. Something we did not have enough of before. I wasn't such a present mother when I was still unhappily embroiled with their father. Now I was able to be the mom I wanted to be, without having to co-parent with someone I had categorical disagreements with on a daily basis.

Our time together became a precious commodity, not something I took for granted. I was beginning to find my strength and to learn that I had power. The power to create a safe haven for my children, and to let them see me grow up before their eyes. From a despairing wife to a single mother. Learning to be strong. Teaching them to be strong, too.

Chapter 3

Homeschooled

As I think about my girls' childhoods, my mind drifts back even farther to my own. Being a little girl myself, running around on the twenty acres of land where I was raised. My parents met in India. My dad was in the Peace Corps in Nepal instead of going to war in Vietnam, and my mom was traveling the world after college, trying to find herself in ashrams. Learning the art of vipassana meditation. Healing what needed healing from *her* tough childhood.

Mom and Dad had my brother in Nepal before returning to the United States during the mid-seventies. My sister was born in Humboldt County, on the Northern California coast. Then came yours truly, entering the world in a log cabin my parents built with their blood, sweat, tears and bare hands. We didn't even have electricity or plumbing yet. Those luxuries came years later. I can still remember the day we had a flush toilet put into the house. It was a big deal. I was about five years old and watched the heavy equipment dig the septic tank hole in the backyard. Before this, we had a rustic outhouse. One where you had to check for large spiders or lizards before you sat down to pee. And did I mention I have a severe

---

A lifetime ago this was my little family. I'm the one in my mother's arms.

case of arachnophobia? Yep. I sure do. My upbringing really solidified that fear for me. You couldn't go an hour in the day without encountering spiders of all types and varying aggressive tendencies. Wasps sometimes entered the house through an open door and dive bombed your head, and alligator lizards, scary creatures looking more like baby alligators than anything else I'd seen, were everywhere. It was the wild west at my place and I wasn't really the "outdoorsy" type.

I was homeschooled through my early years. Which was both a blessing and a curse. The isolation and loneliness I endured living in the middle of nowhere, seven miles from the nearest hint of civilization, was pretty intense. But I liked doing my own thing. When I wanted to draw, I drew. When I wanted to read, I read. I certainly had school work for the homeschooling program I was in, but it wasn't a grueling amount. Just enough to help me not appear to have been brought up by cave people. Enough so that when I did choose to enter the public school system I would not be light-years behind my peers.

Yep, my naked phase started early.

I tried going to school half a year in second grade but was not impressed. All the commotion was such a shock to my system that I did not thrive in the environment and my mom pulled me out and resumed home teaching. I didn't give school another go until the sixth grade. At that time I started attending the school where my father taught music, an hour away from home. The kids were nice. I made friends easily and I was at the perfect age to learn how to infiltrate into society. It went well enough that I stuck with it this time. But I'm thankful for homeschooling. It shaped me and taught me to think outside the box. To this day, I run from conformity. I march to the sound of my own heartbeat and avoid following the crowd. Sometimes people don't understand me because of that, but that's okay.

Chapter 4

NAOMI

To know more about who I am, you need to know more about my nuclear family. First, let me introduce you to my sister. She was a New Year's Day baby; January first, nineteen-seventy-seven. A crazy-adorable kid with chubby cheeks and eyes wide like a fruit bat. Meredith Naomi Walker came into this world with a lot on her mind. As she grew up it was obvious that she was not your everyday American girl. Social justice, feminism, ethical treatment of our environment, were some of many things on her passionate agenda to make this world a better place. She once wrote a letter to Mr. Rogers. He wrote back. They exchanged words as pen pals for six months. They were like-minded individuals. Both good to the core.

But Naomi was not particularly happy. She was rather a tortured soul. Four and a half years older than me, I idolized her to the ends of the earth. As her little sister I wanted to tag along and be her confidant, but she rarely indulged my wants. Most of the time she seemed angry with me, as if I couldn't do anything right. Throughout her short life, she accomplished adventures such as a year of high school at an international

---

During her happy times, Naomi shined her brilliant light so bright.
I love how you can see her joyful, wise spirit overflowing in this picture.

boarding school in India and visiting friends in Bangladesh and South Korea before returning home. She mountain biked across America, worked for Greenpeace on the East Coast, and touched every person she encountered with either extreme charm that induced admiration, or extreme irritation. She had a difficult relationship with men. You might say she was a bit militant in her feminism. Because of her strong female presence, I think most men were threatened by her. Maybe she was just evening the score for all the generations of women threatened by men. Whatever the case, she was a true, beautiful hippie at heart who enjoyed baking banana bread and making unusual herbal salves, arguing with whoever disagreed with her, and adventurous excursions into the wild unknown.

As Naomi grew up and moved out, it was hard to be at home without her. I was dreadfully lonely. Our older brother had flown the coup a couple of years earlier and adjusting to being an only child was hard. Even though my sister and I didn't get along that well, I was very attached to her, and in my teenage years, it would have been helpful to have her around to talk to. There were so many questions I had for her, but I didn't get the chance to ask.

One of my favorite memories is visiting her where she lived on the coast. Arcata, California is so lovely. She lived with several roommates in a little house on G Street. I was sixteen or seventeen at the time. My friends and I had gone to the beach for the weekend and they dropped me off for a night so I could catch up with her. At one point we walked to our favorite store called Bubbles. It was full of the most wonderful smelling soaps, lotions and essential oils on the planet. I bought a small vial of vanilla oil. A little dab on the wrist and the scent is intoxicating. I still have a tiny glass vial of it in my purse, and I can't remember if it's the same one I got that day or if I replaced it in more recent years. Either way, when I take it out and dab it on, I'm back there with Naomi. Making salads in her kitchen, eating with her on her rooftop underneath the Arcata sky.

During my senior year in high school I started hearing my parents speak in hushed, worried tones about Naomi. They didn't explain much to me at the time, but from what I overheard she had recurring fevers and her blood work was coming back with abnormal results.

Some details are now fuzzy, but what never fades is the fear that seized my heart, a sinking feeling of doom. What never diminishes is my love for my sister and how damn much I miss her.

When she was properly diagnosed with leukemia, Naomi was ordered to check in to the University of California San Francisco Hospital (UCSF) to begin immediate treatment. The chemo was brutal. They hit her cancer so aggressively it was as if they were trying to kill her. But the doctors stated, had she not sought treatment when she did, she would have been dead within eight weeks. So here I was, my senior year in high school living mostly in San Francisco with my mom and my sister, trying not to listen to the thoughts creeping into my mind… "What if she dies? What will life be like without her?" I tried to push these terrible thoughts and feelings aside and focus on her survival as what MUST be the outcome. It was entirely too much to consider the many unknowns about her condition. Everything felt unsafe. And, to be honest, I've never felt safe since. Not after the day this unwelcome storm came knocking at our door.

Naomi finished two or three rounds of cruel and relentless chemo. She endured severe blisters in her mouth, her skin basically peeling off in many places, her beautiful curly hair falling out. And yet, on the bright side, she was given the positive news that her body had achieved remission. She had one more round of treatment to go and she would be officially cured of her leukemia. Just one more round! Great, right? Well, that was easy for us to say. We weren't the ones undergoing this extreme medical torture with good intentions.

How I would love to give you the news that Naomi, my stubborn and strong sister, is alive and well today. I would love to post pictures of the two of us hiking just last weekend, or say that she is living an adventurous life overseas. I would love to say just about anything other than the truth, but this book is about the truth, and I don't know what to tell you except for the facts that nearly kill me each time I reflect: Naomi died on May eighth two thousand and one, in her boyfriend's home in Hawaii, from a relapse of leukemia she chose not to fight anymore. She was twenty-four years old. When she learned of her relapse, she was told that a bone marrow transplant would give her a twenty percent chance of survival. It still amazes me that she did not want to give it a shot, but she didn't. No more hospitals, no more spinal taps, no more chemo blisters in her mouth. She chose to quietly slip away from us in relative peace. Mom was in the room with her when she left. I was across an ocean, at home in California, losing a jagged piece of my heart I will never get back.

Chapter 5

Rosemary Hill

There's a hill somewhere in California I used to climb with my brother and sister when we were kids. Up behind my great aunt and uncle's house. The hill smelled distinctly like rosemary. It must have grown wild up there, because whenever someone cooks a meal with rosemary, I'm immediately transported back to that hill with Sid and Naomi.

We once stayed with our great aunt and uncle for ten days while our parents were at a meditation retreat. These are the things you deal with when raised by hippie parents. As I recall, it was awful. The ten day stay, not the hippie parent upbringing. We were young. We missed our mom and dad so much. Aside from memories of that scented hill and the sunshine and dry grass, I recall sliding down the carpeted staircase until my belly got red and raw. Painfully irritated by too much friction. But the entertainment was worth it.

My uncle loved to tease me. He was a huge, intimidating man. Using the word "huge" to describe him is not an understatement. He was six foot five inches tall and not exactly skinny in his older age. Uncle Roy had a dry sense of humor that little girls like me didn't understand. At breakfast one morning I was eating an over-easy egg by picking the whole thing up with my fork and nibbling small pieces. Uncle Roy commented about my being "quite the barbarian." Thinking back, it makes me laugh. What he could have done was just remind me how to use my knife. I was only four or five years old. But what fun would that be for him, right?

That hill with all the rosemary, it stands out in my mind. Climbing up there, the three of us, in the warm glow of the day. The memory feels like happiness. Togetherness. My siblings and me: The Three Musketeers. I don't harbor many of these recollections in the childhood compartment of my brain. So I cherish this one carefully. I want to be able to hold onto it forever.

Chapter 6

My Crazy (Wonderful) Brother

His name is Siddhartha. He was born in the same birthplace as the Buddha. He's a musical genius who plays the fiddle like nobody's business. A real character, a little crazy (literally), and one of my very best friends. He's mostly a big teddy bear with a heart of gold, but on a bad day he makes my blood boil. I guess that's kind of what siblings are for. People in our lives who make us cuss them out like a sailor one moment, and then we make sure to say, "I love you, drive safe" the next. He's a handful by anyone's standards.

He's played fiddle for stars out of Nashville for years. I'm not gonna name drop but he's shared the stage with Rhett Akins (best known as Thomas Rhett's dad now, but a huge star in his own right back in the day), Kevin Sharp (may he rest in peace), Craig Morgan, Jason Aldean, Billy Currington, Andy Griggs, Louise Mandrell, Jerrod Niemann, even Charlie Daniels (may he also rest in peace; so sad he's gone). And, a girl named Arianna V. Khamsaly...wink, wink. Oh my, I just name dropped. I said I wouldn't do that. But that was like a sudden attack of name dropping diarrhea. Sorry (sort of).

My brother, Sid, holding Willie Nelson's guitar named "Trigger."

About a month after our sister died, Sid went off the deep end with some type of mental breakdown. He became noticeably paranoid and freaked-out all the time. It was like I had lost both my siblings at once. My sister was dead and my brother was unrecognizable from who he was before she went away. He had a series of diagnoses, none that really stuck. Through it all I kept thinking, "I don't care what he has, just please let him be happy and not stuck in a nightmarish existence for the rest of his life." He's come a long way. I reconciled a long time ago that he will never be "normal," at least not in the typical societal standard. But isn't being normal overrated? I don't even think I fit the bill, either. Amen to abnormality.

I rarely see him when he doesn't have something to say about a possible alien invasion, or giant insects starting to hatch out of prehistoric eggs due to global warming melting ancient ice. I used to try to talk him out of his ideas, but I've stopped. I actually enjoy hearing his thoughts most of the time, even if they seem startling or far-fetched. I can handle anything he wants to talk about as long as he seems happy when he's sharing his thoughts. All I want for him is happiness.

A typical phone conversation with Sid (or at least one of the ones not involving alien conspiracy theories) often goes something like this:

Sid: "What's going on?"

Me: "Not much, how are you?"

Sid: (Long pause)… "I'm good."

Me: "Good!"

Sid: "So…what's new? What's going on?"

Me: "Well, I'm working hard on the book I'm writing. Making progress."

Sid: "Oh, that's cool. So what's the title? Are you gonna call it, 'I'm Stupid But It's All Okay?'" He proceeds to laugh loudly, proud of his put-down joke. But I laugh too. I can't help it. He always makes me laugh, no matter how silly his words are.

Then he switches gears:

Sid: "So, do you keep your peanut butter in the fridge?"

Me: "Ummm…no...I keep it in a cabinet."

Sid: "All the time?"

Me: "Yes. It makes it more spreadable when I need to use it."

Sid: "Yeah, you're right."

At least I'm right about something in his eyes. Funny guy.

Chapter 7

Gifts I Never Knew I Needed

"Making the decision to have a child - it's momentous. It is to decide forever to have your heart go walking outside your body."
– Elizabeth Stone

I was that girl in high school who swore she was NEVER HAVING KIDS! And I meant it, too. I couldn't figure out what the big deal was about being a mom. It seemed like a whole lot of hassle from my perspective when I looked back on what my mom went through to raise us. As is often the case, life has other plans than those we devise in our own minds. I met my ex-husband the day before I graduated from Trinity High School in the small town of Weaverville, California. I had known his mom for years in our community, and somehow I knew he and I would hit it off when he came home to Trinity County that summer. I didn't know why I knew, I just did. The day we crossed paths we saw each other in about four different places. *What are the odds?* I thought to myself. We were inseparable two weeks later.

I jumped in with no reservations. I think I was trying to run away from my life. My sister was sick already, my parents were about to get a

---

My beautiful girls.

One of my favorite pictures of the three of us.

divorce, my world was falling apart and I clung to Jason as a way to have an anchor in a time that was tearing my heart apart. I was so young. We moved to the coast together. A little town called McKinleyville in Humboldt County. For a time we kind of lived a blissful existence. We walked on the beach every day. Ate big dinners with what little money we had, mostly food bought from the Arcata co-op. Yet, I had more and more of a feeling of doom setting in on a daily basis. The topic of death reoccurred over and over in my mind, and I couldn't turn off the thought pattern. I started having panic attacks that caused debilitating chest pains and shortness of breath. I had Jason drive me to the emergency room once during a particularly bad episode. The doctor told me I was fine, just stressed out and hyperventilating. He said to Jason, "Buy her a beer, why don't ya."

A year into our relationship I became extremely sick. The worst stomach problem I had experienced to date was just not going away. I missed my period and decided I better take a pregnancy test, which came back negative. A week later I was still violently ill. Still no period. I figured I better be doubly sure and as a precaution, took another test, positive it would come out the same as the one I took the week earlier. I looked down at the test on the bathroom counter. What on earth was I seeing? I looked back at the box to check the answer key, I looked again at my test. My face in the mirror became white as a ghost. Why? I felt like my life was over at that very moment. I remember crying all day long. Crying when I told Jason. This was not in my plans. This was *not* what I wanted. I had tried very hard to avoid pregnancy, but apparently pregnancy had not tried a bit to avoid me.

We contemplated an abortion. I felt too young and unprepared to bring a child into the world. We had an appointment with Planned Parenthood and got a host of pamphlets to take home. We read about what we should know, and the frequently asked questions couples have when faced with this predicament. All the while I was consumed with stress and sadness. Even when I thought about going through with the pregnancy, I thought about the state of the planet, global warming, pollution, deforestation. I was terrified that if I had a child, he or she wouldn't have much to look forward to in life. Life on a dying planet.

In the midst of all this, Jason expressed that he really wanted to have the baby. He was coming to the conclusion that he wouldn't feel alright about stopping the pregnancy. Also, I had a conversation with my sister who was living in Hawaii, and I distinctly remember her saying to me, "Well, Arianna, I know if you choose to have the baby it will be a real sweet one." Those words float through my mind, and I am so thankful for them. Thankful that the baby growing inside my belly had a father and an aunt who gave me the courage to bring her into the world. Also, my parents were surprisingly supportive when I broke the news that they were going to be grandparents. That meant more than I can describe in words.

I began months of careful eating, no drinking, and lots of reading up on how to have the healthiest pregnancy any woman could have. I was still petrified about the journey we were embarking on, but I was committed. If we were going to have this baby, we were gonna do it right. We were going to give her the best life we could offer. My motherly instincts were kicking in despite the intense trepidation. Luckily, I had the best example I could have asked for in my own mother, so I was a few steps ahead of the game.

Now let's fast forward to the day this pregnancy came to fruition. It was January Thirteenth, Two Thousand and One. The most incredible little four pound twelve ounce being came into my life. My completely unplanned little gift. The event that I felt would end my life plans, goals and ambitions, became the starting point to the most important aspect of my existence. Her entrance into the world was a little rocky for reasons beyond my control, and we spent some days in the intensive care unit because she was so small and needed extra fluids, but all things considered, we survived a few scary moments and got to take her home on her sixth day outside the womb.

Her name is Chloë, and she is a tall, beautiful college student today. She tells me she loves me all the time, probably more than I deserve. She melts my heart. I love her so completely, and I thank whatever higher power exists that I did not end that fateful pregnancy. I am also exceedingly grateful that her little sister came along two years and five months after her. Against all odds, because my ex-husband had a vasectomy, and we followed the doctor's orders to the T. Yet, surprise, surprise, another pregnancy shortly after. And the doctor, instead of admitting he had given us bad advice for after-care, had the audacity to say I must have cheated on my husband and been impregnated by another man. He said this right in front of Jason. I mean, what if he had been a physically abusive partner? I might have been murdered on account of the doctor's accusations. The doc only said it to try to save himself from a malpractice lawsuit. I admit that it was extra satisfying after giving birth the second time to see that the new baby looked *exactly* like her father. Take that, doc. I should have sent him a picture of her with a request that he pay for her college education.

How did they grow up to be this gorgeous?!

She was born in a water birthing center, because there was no way in hell I was going to try another delivery in a hospital bed. Labor was still excruciatingly hard, but the water helped take some of the pressure off of my body during heavy contractions. I remember holding my second born little girl in my arms, submerging her back and legs in the warm water so she didn't catch a chill, and thinking, "Wow! She's so perfect!" My sweet little monkey Gwen is like a mini Kristen Wiig. No joke. I sometimes call her "Gwen Wiig," when she makes me laugh uncontrollably with her adept comedic antics. She's growing up so fast, stunning like her sister, and gives me a run for my money with her incredible stubbornness. I do believe she may be president one day. Or perhaps she'll play the first female president on SNL. I also think she would be an excellent prosecutor. Given how much she loves to debate and *try* to prosecute me all the time. I often have to say to her, "Gwendolyn, you are not my mother! But I *am* yours, so you better listen to me. Kapeesh?!"

One of my main points in writing about my children is that we can make plans all we want in this life, but when kids want to choose their parents, they're going to choose their parents, and if you're lucky enough to be chosen by kids as wonderful as mine (yes, I'm biased, but yes, it's the truth) all you can do is soak up every minute and give endless hugs and kisses. And sometimes a few death stares when they're mouthing off. Just for good measure. It reminds them who's boss.

Chapter 8

Trinity Tribal Stomp

Once a year in my little hometown something incredible happened. I looked forward to it with eager anticipation. It was called the Trinity Tribal Stomp. A prolific music festival smack dab in the middle of the Trinity County fairgrounds. The normal population of Hayfork is about fifteen hundred people. During a Tribal Stomp weekend it increased exponentially. Huge lines of cars and hippie vans made their way down the normally quiet Highway 3, Hayfork's version of Main Street. You started to see the "locals" with more dreadlocks and Bob Marley shirts than the norm.

The funny thing I realize, as I'm writing this, is that nowadays in Hayfork the so-called hippie population is much higher than it used to be. Year round. It has become an epicenter of pot growing. It's always been part of the "Emerald Triangle," but it seems to be living up to that label more and more in the last few years.

Throughout the thirteen years this festival operated, the organizers, Drew Franklin and his wife, Angel, brought in an incredible array of artists. Michael Franti was on stage before any of us knew who he was. Woody Harrelson gave a speech, and I fucking missed it. Don't know how I could have not prioritized that one. Carlos Santana's brother, Jorge, performed a great show. G. Love and Special Sauce headlined one year. He's the reason that Jack Johnson got his big break. I had always been a huge fan of Jack's, but didn't know anything about G. Love until it was my job to pick him and his band up from the airport.

A girlfriend of mine shared the task. We met them at the Redding airport and brought them to the festival later that evening. And when they finished their sets on stage, we shuttled them back to their hotel rooms in Redding and my friend and I stayed in a room paid for by the festival organizer, so we could wake up early enough to take G and the band to their departing flight. And no, my girlfriend and I did not sleep with anyone in the band. Just want to make that point clear. But I did have fun singing with G. Love while sitting on the sidewalk outside the hotel in the middle of the night. That is a beautiful memory I hold dear.

One of the things I loved the most about the Stomp was the wide array of food vendors that converged every year. It was all vegetarian and all amazing. Everything from Indian Fry Bread to sweet potato fries and to-die-for burritos. Fresh squeezed orange juice, cool refreshing sun teas. It was blissful to spend the day, listen to music, eat, drink, and be merry. It felt like a type of family reunion for me, because so many of our family friends attended. I could never walk more than ten feet without giving or getting a hug from someone I hadn't seen in far too long. Love was everywhere and seemed to multiply when we all inhabited the same piece of land for three days. Tent cities stretched out almost as far as the eye could see. I was thankful I didn't have to camp, though. My childhood property was about fifteen minutes away. Easy enough to stay there for sleeping and showering, then return for another round, well rested and clean.

Drew also brought in a lot of social and environmental activists to give talks, lead ceremonial dances and other activities meant to expand awareness and encourage positive change in our world. It was impactful. These events made me feel hope for the future of the human race. Hope that maybe peace *does* have a chance. So much kindness, so much good will among men, women and children alike. The Stomp was a communal awakening of the collective soul. That was Drew's thing, and he was a pro.

I can't think of any other setting I've been in my entire life where there were more tie-dye shirts or less deodorant. In fact, my sister happened to be much more alternative minded than I was, and I distinctly remember her going through a long "no deodorant" phase. It's possible she wore something natural, but I'm pretty sure she went completely on strike for a good long while. That was Naomi. Always willing to try out something new, especially if it went against societal norms and made others sufficiently uncomfortable. During one year at the Stomp I remember getting there and finding my sister wearing my favorite dress. A flowing frock of deep red with light colored flowers planted all over it. She would often borrow my clothes without asking. It made me soooooo angry.

Thinking about it now makes me cry. It's funny how you can get mad at a sibling for borrowing your clothes without asking, then years later you find yourself with plenty of garments, but you're missing a sibling. You realize that you would happily live the rest of your life in your birthday suit if it meant you could have her back.

The Trinity Tribal Stomp brought in amazing revenue to Trinity County. Also a type of notoriety it never had before. Some of the more conservative members of the community got mad each year when so many "dirty hippies" came through the area. That's what they called them. It was gross to see the disdain with which many of the locals viewed these large groups of visitors. I always felt more at home when this inundation occurred, but some felt threatened. Threatened by what? Too much love and peace? Too much care for the environment? People need to get over themselves. The Stomp was one of the best things to ever happen to Trinity County, and I hope someday we can see it start up again. When it does, I'll be the first one there.

Chapter 9

Oliver

I walked out of the Arcata Co-op after buying something yummy (can't remember what it was all these years later). A tall man with wild curly hair and kind eyes looked over at me, holding the cutest puppy I had ever seen. The creature could only be described as a fluff ball with legs. He had the most adorable expression on his little face. It was a mix of shyness, discomfort, and annoyance. I think he didn't want to be held at the moment. He wanted to be on the ground roaming around and smelling the scents of the parking lot. Perhaps a small child dropped a cookie that had his name on it. Or a vegetarian corn dog.

The man asked me and Jason if we wanted to adopt the precious living thing in his arms. I said, "Oh man, I wish! I'm afraid we're not looking for a pet right now, but can I hold him a second?" In that split, seemingly harmless second, my eighteen year old heart melted. And yep, you know the rest.

Once we got our newfound friend home we let him run around and smell everything in the house, put him out in the yard to pee, and "Poof!" we were parents to our first four-legged child. We named him Oliver Ivan Chowski. It seemed distinguished enough for a dog as incredible as he was. We usually just called him Oliver, or Ollie for short. He was a Chow, Husky, Collie mix. A lovable mutt. I adored him beyond words.

We would wrestle on the living room floor, he would sneak up behind me and bite me with his sharp puppy teeth, and I would scream, "Ouch!" Then he'd act surprised, perk up his ears, and plop down in front of me on the carpet. Smiling wide, with his big eyes and long tongue hanging out, I couldn't stay mad at him. I didn't care if my arms became bruised and people wondered if I was a battered woman in need of help. Oliver was worth it. He was worth the money spent at the vet, worth cleaning up after getting covered in mud when he squeezed through the fence to play with the neighboring wolf-dog, Nakita. He was worth every penny and every hassle. Because Oliver was the kind of dog who gave back so much more than he took.

Over the years, as I gave birth to my girls, Ollie was their faithful guardian. He was so excited to be a big brother. He seemed positive that I had babies exclusively so he could raise them. His gentleness was incredible, especially when compared with his massive size. He grew much larger than I ever thought he would. I used to call him my big moose. He was a gentle giant. All heart.

The problem with pets we love so deeply is that, unless they're parrots or desert tortoises, or perhaps an unusually friendly crocodile, their life-spans just don't compare to most humans. And it doesn't seem fair.

My big moose lived to be fourteen. A very old man in dog years. Towards the end he began to get sores that wouldn't heal and severe hip problems. He also suffered from episodes of paralysis and seizures. It got so bad, I could tell that even getting up from a sitting or lying position was excruciating for him. I would go pick him up from Jason (who was my ex-husband by then: we shared custody of both the kids and the dog) and Ollie could hardly get into my car anymore. Each time I realized that he was getting weaker and weaker my heart shattered into more tiny pieces. How could I say goodbye to one of the best friends I had ever known? We tried many life-saving and life-prolonging options for our loyal four-pawed pal. And even so, the day came when Jason asked me to take Oliver in to the vet and have him put to sleep. He said he just couldn't do it. I was horrified at the thought, but knew I owed it to my beloved pet to be there for him during his last moments, and let him know how loved he was. How loved he would *always* be.

It turned out that it wasn't just me who picked Oliver up that day for his last car trip to town. Chloë and Gwen came with me. They were as horrified as I was about what we had to do, but they, too, felt a sense of loyalty to their lifelong guardian. They couldn't let him go out alone.

The whole ordeal was SO PAINFUL. But we followed through and saw Oliver take his last labored breath while we rubbed his velvety ears and snout and whispered our last I-love-yous. The vet tech offered to dispose of the body, we said no way. We wanted to take him to my mom's property and give him a proper burial. That's what we did. We had a little ceremony. Made a special cross with his name on it. And cried our eyes out. The girls and I buried pieces of our souls when we buried him. A dog such as Oliver deserves nothing less.

Chapter 10

The Woman Who Gave Me Life

She was born in San Francisco to a Polish immigrant and a Scotch-Irish artist. At a young age, her free-spirited father left to pursue a life of selfish gratification, and Nicola and her brother, Konstantine, were without a father for the remainder of their childhoods. Their mother eventually remarried and they were stuck with a cruel, abusive step-father. One who loved to make pancakes with homemade syrup in the morning and beat the kids in the afternoon. Mom says she was extremely unhappy in her younger years, and I can understand why. She also told me she made peace with her step-dad before he died as an elderly man. She said she was able to forgive him for what he did to her. My mom is a very forgiving person. I don't believe I inherited that trait from her. Am I sorry? Not really.

My AMAZING mom.

She's often told me stories about all the places she lived when she was a kid. You'd think she came from a military family. Every year or two she had to acquaint herself with a new school and hope she would form some lasting friendships this time. But it was hard to attach to anyone when she knew it was only a matter of time before she would have to say goodbye and start all over again. Her favorite place she lived, though briefly, was Western Samoa.

As a young adult she was an art major at UC Berkeley. Intelligent and creative, she majored in art with a focus on sculpture. Working at a mobile juice bar called Fruity Rudy's, she supported herself along the way. After graduating college she married her first husband, Raul. They wed in their birthday suits in the Berkeley hills, with the Beatles song, "Here Comes the Sun" ushering in their married life. But all that abundant peace and love at their nuptials melted away quickly. It wasn't long before Raul became physically violent towards his young wife. Breaking her nose and attempting to break her spirit. But Mom's spirit would not be broken. The way she tells it, the last time he came to her house and tried to harm her she told him to leave and if he ever came back, she would kill *him*. She says she meant it, too. It's hard to imagine my sweet, compassionate mother being violent, but I believe her that she meant it. I'm not a proponent of violence, but in this case, I say, *good for her.* She was tired of being a victim and decided to stop the cycle of abuse. If she hadn't made that choice, I may never have been born. I am so thankful to her for being a survivor. She is more unconditionally loving and caring than I could have ever asked for. She definitely wins the Mom of the Universe Award.

In order to give you an idea of Mom's adventurous nature and personality, I will tell you this: she traveled through the entire Middle East as a young woman. By herself. Even stopped long enough to get a bartending job in Afghanistan. She has ventured through more countries than I can keep track of. She's gone to Egypt to ride camels and see the great Sphinx, beheld the Roman Colosseum, wandered through Greece. Fell in love with a mysterious Turkish man during one of her excursions. Had a momentary romance with a handsome stranger she met under the stars at the top of a Mayan pyramid. I remember her telling me these stories and feeling in awe of her romantically exciting youth. She swam with sharks in the waters of Polynesia, and meditated in ashrams of India.

Mom has encountered a lot of people of notoriety. One of her roommates in college was Margo Adler (American author and journalist). She once had a long conversation with one of the Beach Boys. Creedence Clearwater Revival performed at her prom (they all went to the same school). And she beat one of the Creedence boys at a mean game of tetherball. Did I mention she is very competitive with sports? (For the record, I did not inherit her coordination. I can't play sports to save my life.) Country Joe McDonald used to hire her to babysit his kids. She had a conversation with a nice woman sitting next to her at a community presentation in Bolinas, California, only to find out later that the "nice woman" was Oscar winning Frances McDormand. Mom didn't know who she was at the time, but noticed she was "very well spoken" when she got out of her seat and presented to the group. She even witnessed Martin Luther King jr. deliver his "I Have a Dream" speech on the steps of UC Berkeley's Upper Sproul Plaza. I guess it's safe to say that my mom is my hero. She is a superstar on so many levels.

I could not have raised my children properly without her help. She is equally as good a grandmother as she is a mother. We have so much fun together when we visit. Lots of deep discussions and laughter. And when I'm feeling low or anxious, all I have to do is give her a call and she can always talk me down from whatever ledge I'm standing on. Kind and comforting in incredible ways, my mom is the reason for all the best aspects of me. Without her guidance and example, who knows? I may have grown up to be a serial killer.

Chapter 11

Really, Paco?

My eighteen year old mind wondered, "Why do I feel so weird?" We had one of Jason's friends over for the evening. Paco was an odd guy, to say the least, but I tried to tolerate him because he was so close with Jason. We had dinner, then Paco reminded us that he had brought a homemade coffee cake. He made whipped cream to go on top, then served us all a huge piece. We sat on the living room floor, talking and eating. Jason and I were just two crazy broke kids, so we had very little furniture in our place. Hence the floor sitting.

I began to feel rather dizzy. Out of it. And I hadn't been drinking or doing anything else that would make me feel "off." Paco must have seen me looking puzzled, because he asked me if I was ok. I replied, "I feel strange all of a sudden." That's when I noticed a vague look on his face that seemed different. I'll never forget what happened next.

Paco matter of factly told us that he had made the coffee cake with marijuana butter. I thought to myself, "What a fucking *dick*." He said it so casually, like it was no big deal. He claimed he had forgotten he even added it until I said I wasn't feeling right. I didn't believe him. I am convinced he knew what was in that cake when he served me an unreasonably large piece and watched me eat it. Way older than Jason and I, he knew better, he just didn't care. I think it was some sort of sick joke to him. Like extra entertainment for the night, to watch me, this young woman, barely an adult, struggling to sit upright, almost passing out, then running to the bathroom to violently throw up.

I hoped the throwing up would help. I was relieved, thinking I must have gotten most of the effects out of my system and would soon start feeling better. Boy was I wrong. I proceeded to toss and turn in bed all night, feeling my heart trying to beat its way out of my chest.

I honestly thought I was about to have a heart attack. Jason wrapped his arms around me in bed trying to comfort me. It didn't help. I told him I was seriously worried and he might need to drive me to an emergency room. I was so scared I was going to die. I felt like I was endlessly sinking into the mattress. Disappearing.

To this day I don't know if I'm relieved he didn't take me to the ER, or still pissed off about it. I'm aware that we might have gotten in trouble for having a huge amount of pot in our systems, but come on, this was Humboldt County. They probably wouldn't have even batted an eye. And I would have told them the truth, that I didn't know I was ingesting it until it was too late. I'm sure they would have *totally* believed me, right? I mean, no one would make up a story like that just to get themselves off the hook…Ha!

As you may have guessed, I survived that awful, twisted night. I lived to tell about it. Which is obvious to you because of the fact that I'm telling you about it now. Thank goodness I've never heard of a single incident of pot being lethal. But I was off the charts angry when I woke up. Livid that Paco would put me through such a harrowing ordeal without giving me the choice as to whether or not I wanted to share in his stupid pot cake experience. I felt violated. He put me through one hell of a disturbing night, and pretended it was an accident. I admit it's slightly *possible* he had a memory lapse and really didn't recall throwing in the marijuana butter when he was baking his malicious dessert. But my gut feeling is, he meant to serve me without disclosing the special ingredient. How dare he?

I have hung on to a sincere aversion to pot that formed like cinder blocks in my brain that night. Although I'm not opposed to others using it for a variety of reasons (in fact, I'm a big proponent of medical marijuana), pot in all forms is not for me. Yuck, yuck, yuck, and more yuck.

I feel strongly that involuntary drug ingestion of any kind is a type of assault. Even if no one does anything bad to you once you're in your altered state, it's still mind-blowingly unfair.

I wouldn't mind inhabiting my eighteen year old body again, I miss my pre-baby belly complete with a recognizable belly button, but I sure as heck wouldn't want to go back in time and relive that night.

Chapter 12

Weight

I remember being eight years old and promising myself I would limit my food intake for the day to one green apple. Eight years old and I was already on a crash diet. Fuck diets. Fuck diets and the anorexic horse they rode in on. Fuck media that makes women feel inferior to digitally retouched models who eat cotton balls to fill up their tiny tummies. Poor girls. It is a strange obsession that human beings in modern culture have with beauty, being thin, fake boobs. What ever happened to being healthy and happy? Isn't that what real beauty is?

I woke up this morning thinking about what I'm gonna eat today. Thinking about what I'm not gonna eat today. Thinking about how not to be fat. How many calf raises should I do before breakfast? Wanting to cry because I'm still stuck in this cycle of obsession with eating and not eating and working out and sitting on the couch like a lump on a log. I'm *tired.* I don't want to spend the better part of my waking hours panicked about my body. The size, the shape, the fitness level of this thing that moves me around.

Sometimes I feel beautiful. Then there are days when I feel truly disgusting. I hate to admit it. I'd love to say I've reached a point of body acceptance that leads me to loving myself one-hundred percent. But, no, I have not. I'm still striving. I'm still eating and not eating my way through this maze of health versus enjoyment, work versus play, happiness versus despair. I think it's called being human. And I think sometimes it sucks.

I've been struggling with my weight and body image my whole life. I used to look at models in magazines as a kid and hope and pray that I would look like them someday. That was when Victoria's Secret models were actually voluptuous women. I could sorta, kinda envision reaching the goal of sharing a similar look.

Have you seen the models today? Those "angels" on the runway who probably count their meals in tablespoons and wouldn't dare decide they deserved to fill up more than ninety-five pounds in this world. I'm not saying some of them aren't beautiful. Some of them are very beautiful.

But they have bodies of little girls and then fulfill their womanly duties as centerfolds by getting things implanted into their chest cavities.

One thing I don't need is fake boobs. I sincerely hope that, even if I were not blessed with Double Ds, I would not venture down that route. It's crazy, really, how common they've become. Terrible for a lot of health reasons. To each her own, it just seems like a rather sad act of body mutilation to me. Tummy tucks, on the other hand, are fair game and I want one. True fact. Yes, I'm a hypocrite.

Today I woke up to a cool "memory" of mine on Facebook about this plus size "vlogger" (whatever that means) who gives a candid chat about bikinis for bigger women. She made some awesome points. I was inspired again, as I apparently was two years ago when I first shared her video, and then it caused me to think more about my own body and my own happiness.

Also, strange follow-up to my above musings, I was sucked into one of those Nutrisystem ads by Marie Osmond today, and I finally bit the bullet and called in to order the first month of the program. Not because I hate my body, not just because I want to "bust my belly bloat!" But because I'm tired of feeling lackluster about my life goals in general, and weight is a more immediate issue I can, perhaps, control more than I realize.

Update: I'm on my fourth day of the Nutrisystem plan and I'm not on fire about it, but I think it's what I need right now. I've been looking for something to break me completely out of my stagnant and sometimes harmful eating habits, show me some quick results, and perhaps remind me I can cultivate my body to be whatever I want it to be (within reason). I've only lost one stupid pound so far, but hey, I'm pretty sure there's more progress to come.

Update: (2 weeks from above passage) I'm down nine pounds from my highest weight by now. I was already down six pounds by the time I started this diet, but now I've added three more pounds to the tally. I've been loosely following the Nutrisystem diet, but mostly I've just been working super hard to keep my calorie count around twelve hundred per day. It's paying off.

Update: Fucking, fuck, fuck, FUCK! I've put all that weight back on over the past several months. I'm trying Weight Watchers now and have a strong suspicion I will again become aware that it's up to ME, not a program, diet, super strict lifestyle guru. It's up to me. I'm trying hard to figure out why I won't let myself stick to a healthy path. I am an addict. I self-sabotage all the time. I see it. I see it clearly. But I can't stop it. I only feel good when I am depriving myself of food, and that is not often.

I went to a counseling appointment a week ago for the first time in over three years. I hope it might help me shed some old wounds. I want to feel in control of my life. I want to stop living in fear of ending up a huge couch potato. I started going back to the gym last week. Aside from all the icky guys who didn't learn to take turns in the sandbox growing up, I'm liking it. I'm determined to remember what it feels like to be strong, inside and out. Strong like bull…shit? Strong like bullshit? No. Strong like bull.

Update: (Three weeks later) I'm back to never going to the gym. I've been trying to exercise at home about half an hour a day most days, but I know it's not enough. Today I decided to take a day where I would avoid all added sugars. I've pretty much succeeded. Now, if I can just repeat this about three-hundred and sixty more times…

I can never decide how my anxiety about my body started. But I think it came at me from many angles over time. I watched my mom and my sister always dieting and stressing about their weight, so I'm sure I internalized a lot of their body worries. Also, my brother teased me and called me names that indicated I was fat and he thought it was soooooo funny. To top it off, during my teenage years my dad would tell me I was "always eating too much." These are some of the possible family origins of my weight anxiety. But I know I can't blame all my weight issues on my family.

I can easily say that the top thing causing me so much trouble and keeping me from reaching fitness goals is how petrified I am that either A: I will fail if I try again, or B: I will be hungry all the time. And then there's also C: this icky feeling that makes me think I don't deserve to be the size I want to be. It's a self-worth issue. I start to view myself as "fat" and identify with that image way too much. I look in the mirror and all I can see is my double chin looking back. My belly poking out.

One of the things that keeps me up at night is the question of whether I will *ever be even remotely happy with my body again.* I feel defeated lately, more than ever, and it's scary to experience this discouragement without the fire to turn it around into success.

For any of you reading this who suffer from the same issue, I wish you peace with your body. I really do. And I wish the same for me. I just want to let go of negative self images that don't suit me. I want to look in the mirror and see more than my double chin. I want to see the light in my eyes. A truly happy smile, and the strong woman that I am looking back; scars, stretch marks, imperfections and all. I want to be okay with the reflection I see.

Chapter 13

Too Many Obligations

I've been in a *bad* mood this week. Too many obligations, demands and schedules to keep. And I'm dog tired for some reason. I've been trying to remember all my positive thought tactics, but all I can think about is how annoying everything is and how much I want a bowl of ice cream.

Speaking of ice cream, once when I was single, a little after my divorce, the girls were with their dad and I was ready for dinner but nothing sounded good. So I went to the store and bought two things: whiskey and ice cream. I got an odd look from the woman at the register, but doing your own thing often causes odd looks, and odd looks aren't gonna kill you. Whiskey and ice cream might, if ingested every night, but this was one night and on that particular evening, I went home happy.

But today I am not feeling happy. I feel overwhelmingly like a failure in every way. Nothing I'm doing gets me to a completion point fast enough, and I feel strongly that I would be better off crawling into a bear's den (assuming the bear is a friendly individual) and hibernating until a time when I can emerge with a clearer head and a new lease on life. And as an added bonus, maybe I'd come out of that cave twenty pounds slimmer. Yep, that'd be great.

Chapter 14

Mr. No Good

It started out harmless enough. I noticed that he paid extra attention to me compared to some of the other students in my class. I had the capacity to carry a tune, but that was never what he took note of. He would comment on the shirt I was wearing that day, or some other inconsequential detail about my appearance. Telling me how good I looked.

His behavior towards me went quickly from harmless to downright creepy. He would not only comment on my outfit, but now he began "feeling" the shirts I wore. Especially if they were made from a velvet material. He used this as an excuse to run his hand down my back and let it rest firmly as close to the top of my butt as possible. He lingered there. As if I wanted him to touch me. As if I were his to touch.

This was my high school music teacher. Music was my favorite subject in school until I walked into his classroom. My passion for singing started young. It gave me a break in the day to forget about the millions of things on my mind. For a little while I could float away on the wind of a song and feel a sense of harmony. But this man began encroaching on my harmonious time during my school days and it made me angry. He had a reputation around school for being slimy and some girls I knew would laugh it off and say things like, "Yep, that's Mr. No Good for you." But it nagged at me. It was more than simple flirting. I was used to that from men. This was different. It felt like he *meant* something by it. Like he was biding his time until he could get me in his room alone.

I began having nightmares. They were terrifying. Sometimes he would be trying to kill me by putting an explosive device in my house. Other times he just silently followed me and I couldn't find a place to hide. He got into my head and instilled a type of panic in my psyche. I think one of the things that confused me the most is that nothing bad, like truly-crossing-the-line-bad, had happened with him, yet I was petrified that he meant some type of harm to me. I felt sick to my stomach every time I was around him. It wasn't fair. I was a teenage girl, trying to advance my singing skills, and not only did this man not teach me *shit* during the long class periods, he used it as time to fulfill his gross daydreams and desires.

The last incident I experienced with Mr. No Good, before I decided I'd had it, took place outside the cafeteria at my school. I was standing there with a girlfriend on either side of me. I had a large textbook open because we were studying for an upcoming test. All of a sudden, I looked up and saw him walking straight towards me. Slowly. Staring into my eyes as he advanced closer and closer. He stopped right in front of me, kept staring, then tossed a huge piece of candy on my open book. And it wasn't just any candy, it was a red sucker in the shape of overly sexualized puckered lips. I felt the color drain from my face and I froze. Then, without saying a word, he turned and walked away.

My girlfriends giggled, thinking it was silly and a bit odd. But I knew what it was. It was not silly. It could not be explained away as simply odd behavior. It was predatory and gross, and it was meant to single me out more than he already had. Meant to make it clear how he felt about me. It was disgusting and made my skin crawl.

Here's where I have regrets: Instead of going to my principal and complaining about the creepy nature of this stalker-like teacher, or telling my parents and having them deal with it, I gave myself the short end of the deal and stopped taking music. It sucked! Dropping the thing that kept me alive in school was a foreign concept. And in any normal situation it would have been unthinkable. But this was not a normal situation. It was self-preservation.

Years later, as my father was preparing to retire from his music teaching position at my old elementary school, I heard there were plans to hire Mr. No Good in my dad's place. I was livid. I mean, what the fuck?! Elementary school students are even younger and more vulnerable to predatory behavior than high school students. This was not okay. So I marched myself into the office of my old elementary school and requested an audience with the man in charge. He hadn't been the superintendent there for very long. And I hadn't heard the greatest things about him, but in a small town rumors fly as fast as cars on the Talladega track, and you can't always believe what you hear. I told this man who I was and why I was there. I let him know that the children at his school could be in grave danger if he hired a teacher with pedophiliac tendencies in place of my father. All I could do was try my best to convince him that Mr. No Good was bad news and he should not want him close to his students.

The interesting thing about pedophiles in schools is that they are moved around from school to school in hushed tones. Protected like a percentage of dirty priests in the Catholic church. I don't know why, but I suspect it's been going on for centuries. That doesn't make it right. It's fucked up.

As you can probably guess, the principal at my old elementary school did nothing in reaction to my pleading. Well, nothing but hire on the creep in place of my dad. It added insult to injury. I was finally old enough to know how to speak out, and willing to do so, only to find my words falling on deaf ears.

It wasn't until years later that I finally received concrete evidence regarding inappropriate behavior between Mr. No Good and another student from my high school. She was sixteen at the time and he pursued her heavily. She fell in love with him and carried on an affair for many months. Seeing him alone in his classroom, making out. He pressured her many times to have sex with him, but she stood her ground. Not only was he forty-something years old at the time, he was also married. To a woman I adored who also worked at our school.

The incidents with this other girl, unbeknownst to me, happened just before I first set foot in Mr. No Good's classroom. When I assembled all the pieces of the scenario, I wondered in horror if he had been looking for someone to replace his previous young love interest. Maybe he was missing her, missing his extra curricular activities in his locked music room after school. But he didn't bargain for a girl like me when he singled me out. I've been a victim to some crappy male behavior, but I was not going to be *his* victim. No matter how much he hoped I would be. Somehow I saw right through him from the very beginning. I wish the same could be said about all predatory men who passed through my life over the years, but at least this story ended well for me. Not great, but well.

To anyone reading this who has power in a school system. Please do more to protect our school children. They deal with so much as it is, don't make them struggle through victimization in class by a person in a place of authority and influence. Just don't. Make noise if a teacher is found to be harming a student. Risk being fired to do the right thing. If you are fired, continue to do the right thing and warn others of predators. You have a voice. It may not be listened to, as I can attest, but use it anyway and keep trying. Please.

Chapter 15

Funny Things My Daughters Say

My Gwen is always complaining of injustices between her and her older sister. She is convinced everything is tipped in Chloë's favor and that somehow I love and value Chloë more. It's certainly not true. I love them both like crazy and with equal depth and strength.

But because of Gwen's intense belief that I am always treating her sister with more concern, I had to laugh when I ran across something quite clearly skewed in Gwen's favor. I didn't mean to do this, but apparently I have kept way more track of the funny things Gwen has said over the years, and I've only tracked Chloë quotes a small amount in comparison. Sorry, Chloë! You are wonderful and adorable, and this has no bearing on how much I cherish you. And...you're welcome, Gwen, you little rascal, you.

So, here it goes. I am now going to type out the quotes I have kept track of. Or at least the ones that the girls are ok with me repeating. And keep in mind that some of these are more recent and others are from when they were still cute little tykes. I'll make it interesting and not specify. Your imagination can decide the timeline here:

***

Gwen: "Mom! Chloë once shared a popsicle with Miley [the cat]."

Chloë: "Ha! That was when I was really young, *thank you very much*. It was tropical flavor and she loved it!"

***

Gwen: "Even *I* think my farts stink tonight. Was there cabbage in that lasagna??!"

***

Chloë: (Talking about the dog) "Mom! Luna's snout smells good!"

***

Gwen: "I should carry a poison doughnut in my backpack for in case I meet a bully!"

***

Gwen: "I could fend for myself in the wild if you need me to sleep outside."

***

Gwen: "I've never been scared of monsters. I'm just afraid of seeing dead people."

***

Gwen: "I hate that their relationship dynamics bother me so much, but it makes me want to stone an elf. With a rock." (sidenote: should I be worried about her psychological state and elf murdering tendencies?)

***

Me: "Oh my God, do you smell the skunk outside?! It must have sprayed. Or maybe it's the clothes that are in the dryer. They smelled odd when I tossed them in."

Gwen: "No, the dryer never smells like that…(she pauses)...Unless you put a skunk in it."

***

Me: "I guess there's a hormone imbalance that causes PMS way more days of the month than the norm."

Gwen: "Yeah, I know. I think I might have that. But at the same time, it might just be my personality. I kind of think I'm just hungry and mad all the time."

***

Gwen: "I love buffets, but they're *so dangerous.*

Me: (Laughing) "Why? Possible food contamination?"

Gwen: "No, because there's nothing there to stop you from eating too much."

***

Gwen: "Okay, yay! I'm gonna have coffee and go for a run. Just like a suburban mom."

***

Gwen: "Mom, do you know where the power strip is for my room? I mean, not the power strip, but the thing you plug into the wall that gives you more outlets?"

***

Gwen: "Chloë! This is *so unfair!* I am SINGLE PARENTING THE GUINEA PIGS!!!"

***

And lastly, when the girls were super young (yes, I'm giving the time frame away) They used to love the Wizard of Oz and acting out the scenes. I said to them when they received cards in the mail from one of their grandfathers: "Wow, girls, you each got money in your cards from Papa Jim! You're RICH!!" Gwen responded, "No, I'm Dorothy, and *Chloë's Rich.*"

Chapter 16

SINGING

Sometimes when I sing, time stands still. There is no future, there is no past, there is only this one given moment and I am completely blissed out to be in it. Other times, I look out at an unexpressive audience and wonder, *Why am I wasting my time?*

The entertainment industry is a finicky business. I'll never stop singing. It's my life's passion. But some shows lend more life force than others. I used to get terrible stage fright. A long time ago I vowed to myself that if I was going to stay on the performance track, I damn well better learn to enjoy it, because if I didn't, what the hell was the point?

My happy place.

I think singing is my way of sharing the deepest aspects of my soul with others. Often perfect strangers. It feels important. Anything that imparts strong emotions to others seems to have value. Especially in this world that often focuses too much on superficial topics and values. With the advent of Reality TV, our society started to go down the tubes with ignorance, small-minded morals and harmful aspirations. In my opinion, fame at all cost is a disgusting goal. Fame by way of offering a little beauty to the world in the form of music, however? Well, I can feel good about aspiring to this. And don't get me wrong, some Reality TV is great. But a lot of it needs to dig deeper into things that matter. Real reality.

I am excited to announce that I have officially started my second album. Out of the blue I recently got in touch with the woman who sang background vocals for my first album out of Nashville. The one I recorded when my last name was Reiter instead of Khamsaly. A lifetime ago. Her name is Lydia Salnikova and she was one of the members of the Grammy-nominated band, "Bering Strait." She's a multitalented artist and I am over the moon to be working with her again.

I'm a little ashamed to let you know I've been wanting to put out a second album for almost ten years now. That's depressing to admit. Where does the time *go?* But I'm a big believer in the journey, not just the destination. I *will* get there. Eventually.

I've written over a hundred and fifty songs in my lifetime so far, so I'm not a complete flake. I hope. And lately I've been working with a new co-writer here in Redding. He's amazing and for some reason our ideas just click when we write together. Maybe it helps that we have the same birthday. Good old April fourth. We have been charging full steam ahead with a lot of material, and soon we'll be sending some final demos off to a connection I have at Atlantic Records. Crossing our fingers that they'll want to have a few of their artists cut our songs. Stranger things have happened, right? We're also gonna work on releasing material for me as an artist. Exciting!!!

Chapter 17

River of My Dreams

My favorite place on Earth is a secluded beach along a wild river called the South Fork of the Trinity. A beach looking out over the largest swimming hole I've ever encountered in all my Trinity County adventures. This piece of serenity is where I spent a good chunk of my childhood every summer. It is hallowed ground. Holy water running through a deep ravine.

Up the mountain from the river was where my parents' friends, Brian and Cindy, lived. In an old mining cabin that hadn't been confiscated by the government. Surrounded by fruit trees and fertile gardens, there was vitality and new life everywhere you looked.

This favorite spot of mine was where Brian and Cindy would hold "family gatherings." I put it in quotes because mostly we were one big family of friends, not blood relations. A shocking number of the nicest people you could hope to meet would converge on a Thursday or Friday afternoon, park above the steep trail to the river, and haul huge ice chests, watermelons, fully cooked lasagnas with freshly made pesto, you name it and it was probably in someone's cooler and generously ready for the taking. We all pitched our tents, put our food in the outdoor kitchen and proceeded to rip off our clothes and jump in the cool, clear river of rejuvenation.

Thinking back on it now I realize that this is the closest I've ever come to being baptized. I swear that river is healing, both to the body and spirit. And the fact that we didn't have to wear swimsuits sounds questionable, but it was really quite innocent. No one ever came on to me there because they had seen me naked. I was a beautiful young woman yet felt safe around all these men I had known my whole life. It's a foreign concept to me now. I haven't skinny dipped in a group of people in ages, and I don't think I would feel comfortable having my daughters do this, which is odd to admit, given the fact that I have nothing but wonderful memories from these gatherings, but I guess parenting changes us. What was okay for us as a child doesn't always feel okay for our children.

At night during these mini vacations on the beach, we would light a bonfire, roast marshmallows, and tell stories, sing songs and soak in the authentic love palpable all around us. There was no judgement I can recall, no one trying to be the leader of the pack (well, maybe one guy once in a while, but I won't name names), mostly just communal appreciation of what we were all lucky enough to experience in that place at that time. It seems like we were acutely aware of how unusual these experiences were. They were perfect. Not many things in life are, but these gatherings were.

As I fast forward in my mind, I recall attending a women's gathering on this very same beach. I was with my soon to be mother-in-law, whom I'd known since about the age of ten. This was right after I found out I was pregnant and a couple months before her son and I got married. She was, and is, very dear to me. I am thankful to say that we will remain close for the rest of our lives, even though I am no longer with Jason. But during this particular time, we were experiencing some disharmony. It stemmed from the fact that once she found out we were pregnant, she was overjoyed, but her joy quickly turned to panic because we were not yet married.

Jason and I had plans to marry, but maybe a few years down the road. To his mom, this was not acceptable. She said the elders in the family just wouldn't understand or approve. I was torn about this whole issue. I look back and realize that my intuition was telling me I shouldn't marry at all. Not while I was so young. But I was impressionable and easily caved to the pressures of others.

So, in the midst of this confusing angst I was experiencing, we ladies went to sleep in the open air on the beach that night, under the bright stars. At some point during my deepest sleep I had a dream. It was one of those "waking" dreams, where the sleep world and the real world merge and you get confused about which is which. I dreamed that I awoke in my sleeping bag, still on the sand, and I was terrified to find an enormous mountain lion crouching over me, with his face right up in front of mine. His eyes were huge and fierce, full of power. As I panicked, thinking this might be the last moment of my existence, the wild cat let out an incredibly loud shriek. It was like an imminent warning and I immediately startled awake, for real this time. Wide eyed and scared in the cold, misty air of dawn. I knew what the dream meant. I knew what this beast of a wild animal was trying to tell me. It was telling me not to go through with the marriage. I knew this, but sometimes knowing something is not the same as being courageous enough to stand up to pressure, or the constructs of convention. Knowing something does not always equal doing the right thing for yourself.

I don't regret having married Jason. I'm very thankful for our children. I just still find it odd that I knew something was wrong all along, but I couldn't stop the plan already laid out for me. As I get older, I purposely lay out my *own* plans. Because if I don't, someone else will, and that someone will not be me.

I am so thankful for that special river refuge, for all the joy it brought into my life. I am older and wiser than when I swam along its shores, but the wisdom I have acquired is partly *because I swam along its shores.* I am in its debt, and I hope we meet again someday.

Besides which, with all the sins I've committed since then, I'm gonna need to be re-baptised.

Chapter 18

I Am Soooooo Not a Brick Wall

Sometimes it seems like my feelings are too big for me. Like an X-Large T shirt that hangs shapelessly on my body. Not doing my appearance any favors. Today I've been consumed with feelings of discouragement and sadness. Out of the blue my whole attitude went downhill, and I haven't been able to pull myself out of my wallowing hole just yet. I experience every feeling as if it's on steroids. When I'm happy, I tend to be *super happy!* And when I'm blue people around me can take one look and tell how down I am. My eyes say it all. I wondered for ages why I cried uncontrollably at every single funeral I ever went to, whether I knew the person being honored or not. I thought something was wrong with me. Until I read an article about people (a small percentage of the human population) who feel *extra* emotions compared to most. I read the ways to diagnose myself. I wanted to see if I was one of these super sensitive human beings. Every aspect was spot-on.

This doesn't mean I'm some special person who exhibits compassion every second of my waking life. What it means is that my feelings are hyper-sensitive. So, when I see someone crying, I cry. And when someone says something even remotely funny, I laugh too loudly. And when I'm in a room full of people saying goodbye to a loved one I've never met, my tears fall as if the departed was my best friend. I am some sort of emotional sponge, an empath, that takes in all the emotions around me without a filter. The side effect of this aspect of my nature is that I end up appearing emotionally unstable and weak beyond description to those who are not ok with displaying their own inner feelings. But I would rather appear silly to some, and be able to extend intense compassion to those who need it, than behave like a brick wall. Brick walls think they're so cool, but the critical side of me thinks they're really just missing out on life while they maintain that stoic facial expression.

Life is too short to have anything left unsaid. For parents estranged from children they may not have been able to raise, reach out. That child, no matter how old, still needs you. There's still a chance that love can find a home between the two of you. And for siblings who no longer speak to each other because of a feud, unless one of you has proven that you really don't care about the other, why don't you try to make peace? It could be healing. And we never know the outcome of any given situation unless we are brave enough to walk through the flames of anger and hurt, to reach the other side of understanding.

Look at me preaching, when I myself have tons of problematic flaws. But I'm preaching to me as well. I always have room, even with my overly sensitive emotions, to be more compassionate, more empathetic, more of an example for others to follow. I will try. And I will keep trying. And I'll continue to cry too much and laugh too loudly and say things most might hold inside and keep to themselves. And that's okay. You may find it silly or abrasive, or even downright inappropriate and annoying. I don't mind. Because I can handle some criticism, but what I cannot handle is going through life with a mask on my emotions. I prefer to let my feelings run wild through fields of colorful flowers. Dancing on the wind of the bees' wings as they gather their pollen. The honey they make will taste like freedom. I will put a spoonful in my morning coffee and I will smile.

Chapter 19

Fuck Math

I recently finished another semester as a student at the community college where I work. I barely passed my Math 101 course I was obligated to take. In fact, I'm currently getting tested for a possible learning disability in the realm of mathematics. I'm not sure they're going to pinpoint a disability, but I am certain that strong disdain and irritation can easily be spotted between me and math. I mean, what the heck? When someone isn't naturally good at music, do we diagnose them with a "music disability?" If we are going to go down this road of "academic disabilities," shouldn't we level the playing field and hold all parts in high regard? But we don't. We don't care if a student is bad at painting or singing, bad at drawing or piano, we don't care if someone can't hold a tune to save their life.

What we care about here in America is whether someone can decipher what the hell 12a - x -14x + 6a - a = 6xa means. Don't try to solve this problem, it's fake and I'm bad at math, remember?

I'm starting my last math course (Math 102) for my associate degree next month. And I feel like I'm about to break out in hives all over my body, and especially in my brain.

Update: I am now miserably and fully immersed in said Math 102 course. I just took a test and got another C, but I passed again.

Update: It's worse than I thought. A couple weeks have gone by and I just got 1 out of 10 on my homework quiz and 1 out of 5 on my syntax quiz. Fucking *FUCK*. Math makes me cry and want to eat my feelings. It makes me feel ashamed of my intellectual abilities and I hate feeling like this. I'm going to get some tutoring this week which I hope will help. Seriously wondering to myself, "Do I really need to graduate this May or should I just drop this class and call it good?"

Update: Okay, it was a harrowing experience to say the least, but I passed Math 102 with another C, I feel utterly inept and stupid, and on that note I am now officially, permanently breaking up with all higher-level math. I am not sorry. I am not ashamed. I will no longer stand for being bullied by numbers that inappropriately mingle with letters. Good *riddance*.

Chapter 20

You Know That Saying, "I Almost Died Laughing?" Well. . .

The last time I ever went swimming with my sister was a lifetime ago. We were at that special spot in Hyampom, and I don't recall many other people there at the time. It might have been the last day of a women's gathering. Naomi and I jumped in the water to cool off and we swam all the way out across the huge pool, looking down at the fish moving far below the surface.

We treaded water for a while, talking. Then something struck us as funny. I wish to God I could remember what it was. I suppose it was something one of us said and it induced sudden giggling. I laughed, she laughed. We both started laughing at the same time. Before long we found out that the harder we belly-laughed, the more we began to sink. We tried to stop because it was kind of freaking us out. Each almost going all the way underwater when our lungs humorously expelled their precious air.

This moment is so crystal clear in my mind I really am surprised I can never recall what set off our giggling. Uncontrollable. Joyful. A little scary under those circumstances. Somehow we finally made ourselves stop and swam back to the sandy beach. Not drowning after all. Our keen senses of humor did not betray and sink us all the way.

On that day, in those particular rays of sunlight, we were both happy mermaids with an instinct for survival, and wild laughter that echoed off the jutting cliff sides above us, where the eagles built their nests.

Chapter 21

I Miss That SpongeBob Laugh

A few years back I was hired at an elementary school to work in the Special Education Department as a one-on-one aid to a child with autism. I learned many things about children, about myself, and about some of the behavior that presents itself in individuals on the autism spectrum.

At first I loved my job. It was taxing, but my student and I got along great and he was so much fun to work with that the position seemed very rewarding. Over time, however, I came to the disappointing realization that I had been experiencing a "honeymoon" phase, and as my student grew more and more used to me, he began to exhibit his most difficult behavior. My *goodness,* was he stubborn. He dug in with impressive tenacity when he wanted to get his way, which happened to be all day every day. A brilliant child he was, and I loved his intellect and thought processes, but I was not good at brushing off his combative, argumentative tactics. I made the fatal mistake of taking a lot of them personally, and once that cycle began I started to experience health problems associated with the stress of my job. My jaw seized up almost constantly because I was unconsciously grinding my teeth with exasperation during work hours and in my sleep. I was continually drained, both emotionally and physically. And, to make matters worse, when I finished my one-on-one work each day, I jumped right into my after-school aid position duties. No grace period, no break, just kids, kids, kids, and more kids!!!

I was working full-time and barely supporting myself and my daughters. This was the one and only time I tried renting my own house as a single parent. I wanted so badly to provide for my girls and have a place that was their own. But I was drowning in the process. And I needed to rely on my mom far too often to help buy groceries and fill my gas tank. My entire paycheck was only twelve-hundred dollars a month.

The silver lining of working for this particular school was the fact that it was the one my daughters attended. It was an incredible blessing to see them during lunch breaks and playground time. It gave me comfort to be on campus if they needed me. It also ripped my heart out during times they spent a week with their dad and had to leave me at the end of the day to hop on the bus. There would often be tears for all three of us. I hated it. I felt like I was continually abandoning my own children and it felt so counterintuitive to their emotional health. I don't miss those days for that reason.

My day-to-day activities in the special needs department were quite the roller coaster ride. I was assigned to my main student but sometimes worked with other students in need of extra attention and supervision. The other student I worked especially closely with was one who was so darned endearing it was surreal. He loved to laugh like SpongeBob and call me Sandy (like the odd squirrel with a southern accent who hangs around Bikini Bottom in a spacesuit). He wore brightly colored gloves just for fun and played pretend games. And he had a very unusual way of speaking that was so matter-of-fact it fascinated me.

There is one afternoon that lives in infamy in my memory. My two students sat on either side of me at an event in the school gym. There was a speaker up on stage and I was trying to make sure we stayed quiet for the duration of his talk. Out of nowhere one of my students turned to me and said, "Hey, those are nice, *large* breasts you've got there." While the one on the other side of me jumped up, holding his crotch tightly and ran out of the building. I, of course, could not take time for my shock to diminish, I was in the Twilight Zone. First I had to tell the seated student that what he said to me was not appropriate. He was truly shocked when I had to break it to him. Then I was off and running after the kid who escaped from the gym.

I think back to this time and it sure makes me laugh. Not in any sort of demeaning way towards the students. They were just being kids. And kids do say and do the darndest things, right? But I laugh at how funny daily life can be, no matter where you work or who you're with. Life is just *funny.* And it's a damn good thing that it is, because if it weren't it would just be all pain all the time.

Eventually the aunt of one of my students started coming in every day and picking apart every single thing I did while working with her nephew. She apparently decided I was completely inept and that she could do a better job. So she tried to have me fired, and instead I said, "I'm done." Luckily I knew I had been a good employee. The principal at the school was happy with the job I did and so was the special education teacher I worked with every day. That's what mattered to me. All I could do was all I could do. And that's what I did, until it was time for me to move on.

I think about those two students often. I miss our good times together. One of them still lives nearby and we run into each other once in a while. He's a towering young man now. And quite a budding actor. A kind soul. The other moved down to Southern California a long time ago, but once in a blue moon I receive a message or a phone call from his mother, letting me know he was asking about me. There is an old voicemail I keep on my phone. It's from him, and he is wishing me a happy New Year. His sweet nature is so dear to me. I hate that we don't get the chance to visit in person anymore.

You couldn't pay me to go back to that position, but I wouldn't be who I am today without that intense learning experience. It was an education in human nature and the amazing ways personality traits present themselves. I believe a lot of children with autism become adults who change the world. Brilliant and unique blessings to be appreciated and honored. I look forward to seeing what my former students choose to do with their lives!

Chapter 22

Plenty of Fish

His picture flashed across my computer screen. Damn. I thought to myself, *"He's really handsome."* But I was stuck in a cycle of despair. Still convinced I would never love another man again. So I didn't contact him. Not a word. A couple days passed. Guess what I found in my inbox? A message from this handsome face with the mischievous eyes staring back at me. Wow. Maybe this was what love at first sight felt like? I messaged back.

As we continued to communicate, I found that we appeared to be complete opposites but with very similar outlooks on life. Out of the blue a couple days after messaging, he called me. I was amazed. He sounded nice. He talked about football. I said I wasn't a football fan. He said, "You will be when you watch a game with me." I thought that was funny, but implausible. But guess what? I'm a bit of a football fan now, because watching it with him really IS fun. His passion for life, his joy in movies he's already seen a hundred times, his amazing smile and happy eyes. He's the love of my life and I'm shocked that we found each other. Someday we need to do an add for the POF dating site.

The only reason I found myself trying out online dating in the first place was because a dear friend encouraged me to give it a go. She saw how much I was struggling with a recent breakup and said, "You know, Arianna, I know you're not wanting to get back into a relationship anytime soon, but I really think you should try online dating. It might cheer you up a bit and remind you that there are nice guys out there." At the time I told her she was crazy, but now I am so thankful for her matchmaking skills. I never would have met Lefty if it weren't for her encouragement.

Yes, my fiance's name is Lefty. It's quite the conversation starter. His given name is Leutvilay, but the nickname of Lefty stuck in third grade when his teacher couldn't pronounce his name, so instead of doing the right thing and trying harder, she simply called him something else that made her life easier. And yes, he is left-handed. Like President Obama. And like my mom and my older daughter. Also my sister. She was a left-hander too.

Even though I think Lefty's third grade teacher was culturally insensitive, and should have called him by his given name, I love that he goes by Lefty. At first glance it brings so many questions to mind: Is he a mobster? A cowboy? Is he the Lefty from that famous Willie Nelson song? He's a man of mystery. And he has mysteriously stolen my heart. I have the strongest feeling I will never get it back.

Leutvilay is from Laos. He came to America as a little boy with his family. First they lived in Sacramento, then a few years later they moved up to Redding. He is a beautiful example of someone who assimilated into American culture flawlessly while preserving his own culture and language of heritage. He is a strikingly good person. The kind of guy who drops everything to fix a niece's car or carry a large piece of furniture for an elderly neighbor.

I lucked out with the online dating scene. It's still surreal. I look over at Lefty and I can't believe how amazing he is. He's the one I spent my life searching for, and now he's mine and I'm his.

Chapter 23

Nine to Five

Working too much at conventional jobs feels like poison being administered directly to my overly sensitive soul. I'm always telling myself I'm lucky to have a job that pays the bills. I'm fortunate to have good secretarial skills that make me easily employable. But am I lucky? Or just unhappy. Pretty sure I'm just unhappy.

I've never fit in to the workaday world. I've always despised it with a passion, partly because I know there is so much more to life than meets the eye. I want to find a way to live on my own terms and stop living by everyone else's rules. Maybe I just never grew up. Maybe I'm just a woman with the mind of a spoiled child, but something tells me that's not what it is. This voice often whispers to me that I'm on the wrong path, but I have yet to figure out how to get on the right one. I've had glimpses of it. I know where the trailhead is. I know *exactly* where it is. I can sense I'm running out of time. I need to make a run for it soon. Can't waste away at a desk forever. I'll be six hundred pounds in ten years...Damn donuts in the break room.

I'm going to a training day next week for work. I was kind of excited about the topics to be covered, until I discovered I had to choose between the two I was most interested in, because they're booked at the same time. So, I either get to learn about my rights as a worker, or do a guided meditation and yoga seminar aimed at reducing stress. It's tragically a bit comical: learn my rights or learn how to not die of a heart attack due to a crazy work environment. Isn't one of my rights the right to not die of a heart attack due to a crazy work environment? My mom laughed when I told her about this dilemma and she said she'd give me a complimentary yoga and meditation class whenever I want. She used to be a yoga instructor, and she's been a lifelong, devoted meditator, so I may take her up on that offer.

Update: I ended up saying "screw it" and went to the above-mentioned meditation and yoga seminar. It was great! I decided I can study up on my "rights and responsibilities as a worker" another time. Like when I'm dead.

Today my coworker asked me how late I was on shift, and I told her five p.m. Then I added, "Unless I run screaming before then." She laughed. I laughed noticeably louder. Also, today I interviewed for a new full-time position at the main campus of the community college. I'm pretty excited to announce I gave the best interview of my life to date. I know I rant about conventional work a lot, but I do get excited about the possibility of positive change. This position would mean a better income, health insurance so I can get off of Medi-Cal, and way less commuting. Would I rather be a full-time singer/songwriter? Yes. Am I aware that I owe it to my family to bring in a responsible adult income? Yes. Is this kind of a dream-crushing conversation to be having with myself right now? Yes.

Update: Fast forward three days from the above statement about my interview: Apparently giving a first rate interview didn't cut it. I received a call today informing me I was not moved forward to round two of the interview process. The call would have been harder to take if it did not come from such a nice human being. The man who contacted me was the head of the interview committee. He was incredibly kind and seemed apologetic. I couldn't help but feel he was one who voted for me to move forward, but maybe I'm just deluding myself. I told him, "Wow, I'm disappointed to hear this. Can you tell me why I was not moved forward, for future reference?" He said that, without breaking any confidentiality rules, what he could tell me was that it was a highly competitive field of applicants and mostly it came down to education level.

Ouch. That kind of hurt, but I understand it. I'm so close to finishing my Associate's degree, but for all I know most of the other applicants probably had their BAs and/or Master's degrees. I can't compete there. And is it silly for me to admit that I don't *want* to compete in this capacity? My time in life is precious. It has taken so much over the years just to be this close to my *two-year degree*. When I'm finished with this goal, I'm done. I will not study my life away in order to appear more qualified for jobs on paper. I know my worth as an employee and my rebellious nature is prominently reminding me that I'm good enough as I am. Take me or leave me. No one else knows the struggles I've overcome in life, as a young mother, as a single mom all these years. I'm kind of a superstar as a mom, and a Master's degree would neither detract nor add to that fact.

Update: I completed a total of three new job applications yesterday for more main campus positions. Crossing my fingers that one of these pans out and I can stop commuting too much and living too little. I'm especially interested in acquiring the position in the Step-Up Department. The Step-Up program helps ex-convicts shed their societal stigmas, make goals for their future, and acquire new educational skills. That would be amazing!

Update: (*Sigh*) I was not chosen for any of the above-mentioned positions. Am I too blonde? And do I even fucking care at this point? Here's a hint: No.

Chapter 24

Nashville, How Do I Love Thee? Let Me Count the Ways

My plane touched down and I knew I had landed in my second home. I was visiting my brother for the first time in Nashville. He was playing fiddle for Craig Morgan and arranged for me to see their show at the Crazy Horse that night. I watched by myself, fending off strange men who tried to buy me drinks, but I had a great time. And I was such a proud sister, watching Sid up there on that big stage.

It wasn't until several trips later I was able to record my Nashville album. I flew in, listened to the songs my brother picked out for me, learned them for a day, then spent the next day in the studio with a full band. We hung out with the songwriter legends who were kind enough to let me record their work. It was an honor to meet them all. This was before I became a songwriter myself.

One of my best friends, Jim Hyatt, co-produced my album alongside my brother. Jim also played bass for the tracks. He's a studio musician, painter, producer, songwriter, chicken farmer, goat herder, dog lover. A man of many talents and interests. I've run my songs by him for years, valuing his opinion. A favorite memory is one night at Losers Bar when Jim pointed to an unassuming man with long grey curly hair like Bach. He said, "See that guy over there? He wrote *Friends in Low Places* for Garth." I loved the fact that there were legends around every corner of the city.

One day Jim introduced me to a friend of his named John Goodwin. A talented artist in numerous areas: painting, 3D art, songwriting, cracking dry humored jokes, being weird. He's a unique individual who makes you think a little harder about the questions of the universe. Legend has it he used to be a mentor to Alanis Morissette. His songs have appeared in soundtracks of Jeff Bridges movies like "Crazy Heart" and "Surfs Up." Jeff is John's childhood friend since the fourth grade. They're still good pals. I've always thought it would be fun if, while visiting John, Jeff walked through the door and had a beer with us. Hasn't happened yet, but here's hoping. Last time Lefty and I were in Nashville we had a great visit with Mr. Goodwin. And he was nice enough to send us off with one of his signature creations. A poster with his saying that goes like this:

Verse

Chorus

Verse

Chorus

Lunch

Bridge

Chorus.

This illustration of a typical songwriting session hangs in major music studios on Music Row.

After seeing Sid perform with Craig Morgan that first time, he and I went to have some drinks on Broadway. It was New Year's Eve, so we wished each other a "Happy Naomi's Birthday" at midnight and had whiskey on the rocks in honor of her. The bar we chose was packed tight. I looked up at the tiny stage to see John Rich and Dierks Bentley doing an impromptu performance. I'm sure the bar paid them to "drop in" unexpectedly and surprise their patrons, but it was still exciting. What a great introduction to a city that has part of my heart and at least half of my soul. It never loses its luster. Every trip I take there is an adventure. And someday I'm determined to sit down with a major songwriting publishing group and be told, "Yes, we want you on board." "Yes!" I like the ring that word has to it. A publishing deal and a co-write with my idol, Brandy Clark, will someday make my world complete. I believe, I BELIEVE! Thank you *JESUS!!* (Maybe I should order that 'Miracle Spring Water' from the psycho on TV to expedite the process. I bet if I do I will suddenly win a million dollars and the painful rotator cuff problem with my shoulder will be healed.)

Chapter 25

Aging As a Woman (Or, I Have No Expiration Date, for Fuck's Sake)

I looked in the mirror today and noticed a new line on my face. It looks like a tiny paper cut that doesn't bleed, located at the edge of my mouth on my right side. It slants slightly downward. I don't think it was caused by smiling. Pretty sure it's from one too many frowns.

As a woman I've been taught that I lose value as I age. I've been told a million times in a million ways that each minute passing robs me of a part of my desirability. My sex appeal. Even though I know so many of these negative messages come from corporate ad campaigns trying to sell me something, or from shallow and un-evolved misogynistic men, I can't stop them from getting into my head. I keep them at bay as much as possible, but it's a daily struggle. And the struggle wears on me.

Almost everywhere we look we see messages telling women they are not good enough, will never be good enough, and have been fighting a losing battle since the day we were born. I remember being in Nashville a little while after I released my first album. My brother and I ran it by a music industry executive in a meeting, checking the viability of a record deal. The guy listened to some of my songs, asked me some questions, and said something I will never forget:

"How old are you?"

"I'm twenty-eight," I answered.

He put on his pensive expression, cocked his head to the side like an Australian Shepard, and said, "Okay, well, you're not *quite* too old to be signed to a deal yet."

His words still ring in my ears. They live inside my head, even though I should have murdered them with my bare hands a million times over. I'm now thirty-eight years old. Does this mean in that music executive's eyes I'm supposed to be living off of creamed soup and oyster crackers and drinking Ensure while I pass the time in my room at the old folks' home? Our societal obsession with a woman's age is designed to keep female human beings down. Concocted to make us feel like we already had our shot and it didn't pan out, so we might as well give up now. There are sooooo many things wrong with this line of thinking. It makes me angry as hell.

We tell men as they age that they only get more distinguished. We tell them they are more mature, they've learned how to perfect their lovemaking skills, they look *good in that gray hair.* As I think about this topic, I realize that these discrepancies go far deeper than age. For instance, when a young teenage girl decides to send a nude photo to the boy who has been bugging her for one for days, he then shows it to all his friends and the whole football team. She is mortified, called a stupid slut by everyone at school, and what happens to the boy who originally asked for the picture? He becomes a god among high school boys. He's so cool. He's a player. Look what he was able to get a girl to do for him. He's got *swag.*

Please excuse me a minute while I go vomit multiple times.

We have a long way to go towards any semblance of real equality of the sexes. Sometimes it keeps me up at night wondering if we'll ever get there. I want to be given the same chance, looked at with the same seriousness by a record label as a thirty-eight year old man. Why is that such a radical request? I don't have an expiration date. So don't fucking treat me like I do.

I think one of the main reasons society tells women they are not attractive or desirable past the age of twenty-five is so we won't strive for so much out of life. It makes it harder for us to find and put to good use our true power. A patriarchal society does not want powerful women, it wants pretty girls. Pretty girls who keep their mouths shut and their legs open.

During this inescapable aging process I guess you could say I've gone through some stages of grief when it comes to the best laid plans I made at eighteen. I was going to graduate high school, move to Nashville and do whatever it took to become a famous singer. I could see it so clearly. That time in my life was twenty years ago now; it's hard to believe, but it's getting easier to understand. Bonnie Raitt didn't get a record deal till she was forty-four. I remind myself of this fact daily. It's my mantra. I tell myself I don't have to be on the same time frame as everyone else. And to be honest, I'm finally starting to believe it.

Another thing that changes as I get older is, I find myself rethinking the idea of a record deal altogether. I want to perform but also market my songwriting, maybe get a songwriting publishing deal, then sing live and sell my own albums when I want to, and *only* when I want to. I don't like being told what to do, and a record deal sounds like it would involve a lot of that. For every scenario, there is a middle ground. My middle ground is a publishing deal for my songs and a great band to perform with one weekend or two per month. I'm not giving up, I just don't want the same things as I did when I was eighteen. Shocking, right?

My big picture as I strive to grow older with grace and dignity intact, and yes, even smoking-hot sex appeal, is to keep cultivating the best version of me. My power only grows stronger as I age. My primal growl more fierce. I am a panther pacing in the jungle of twisted vines and false paths, waiting for my perfect time to pounce. To claim what is mine. What has always been mine. Waiting until I find the one path as real as I am. And nothing can stop me. For I've already set the dominoes in place. Now watch me work. Or join me on the prowl. I like company.

Chapter 26

Body Image

I've been working hard to understand my deeply ingrained emotional need for too much food. And I'm trying to figure out what size I want my body to be. Mostly I want to know why I eat so often even if I'm not hungry. It causes me a lot of pain and stress. Especially about my health and shape. Stress that is often debilitating. It stops me from wanting to go to the gym because I feel like I don't *deserve to be there* unless I've been eating carefully in the days leading up to it. What a weird way to think, right? Aren't I working out to *get* in better shape? Why do I feel like I need to already *be* in shape to show my face, and my tummy, at the gym?

I swear, the shit we women put ourselves through on the daily. We can be positively cruel. When I was around twenty-three years old I got in the best shape of my life. I was a size four, about seventy pounds lighter than I am now. I remember I was exercising two or three times per day, eating very little, and drinking a lot of protein shakes. I was still breast-feeding my younger daughter which also helped my metabolism. I nursed my babies a lot longer than the American standard. Chloë until two, and Gwen until two and a half. I think at the time I underestimated how many extra calories are burned making breast milk. The interesting thing about this time in my youth is that I still didn't allow myself to feel good about my body. Even at that size I obsessed about my stretch marks and other imperfections all the time. Day and night. They say youth is wasted on the young, and I've found that to be painfully true.

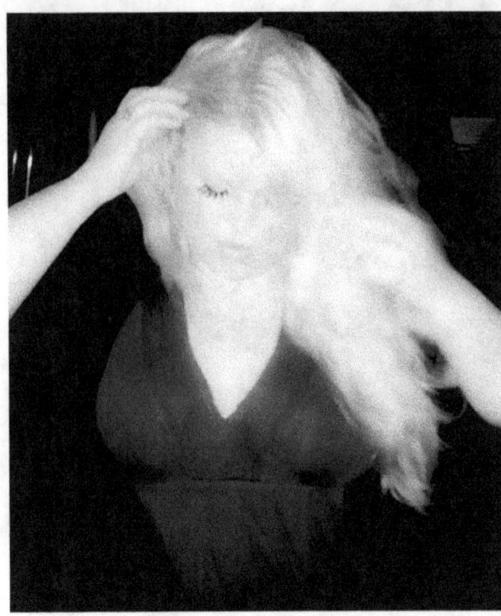

Sometimes I feel found.

But now, all these years later, I want to understand my emotional eating and self-sabotage issues. I want to finally know why I do what I do. I think the only way I will ever change things is if I obtain true understanding. I wish our society could help women to feel better about doing what we need to do for ourselves, without making us feel like we all have to fit into a cookie-cutter shape of conventional beauty. We are making progress. But let's keep going. Marching forward with thick thighs and our heads held high. We are strong. We have curves. We exist. We are beautiful!

Chapter 27

Writer's Block

There are times when the words flow like wine in Italy, and then there are times when words…wait, words? What are those? I've been struggling with a bit of writer's block lately. But I've been writing a ton of new songs, so maybe my comment is deceptive. Life has been crazy. The girls and my step-son, Cameron, just went back to school. Lefty and I are parenting three growing teenagers. Time *flies.* I drove Chloë and Gwen into school this morning, Cam wanted to take the bus with his friends, and I am now sitting on the couch in my pajamas typing away, in denial that I'm gonna be late for work if I don't start picking out clothes to wear. Wait, clothes? What are those?

Last week, for the girls' first day of school, I crawled out of bed, eyes half-open, and said: "Okay, girls, I suppose I'll put on pants and be the *cool mom* while I take you in." Actually, I lied. I put on leggings instead. Leggings are a gift from God.

Chapter 28

Little Girl, Big Worries

Like I said at the beginning of this book, I was born at home, in a six-sided log cabin my parents built. For six-hundred dollars. My mom always reminds me that they followed the pattern advertised in *Mother Earth News*. We were on twenty acres of isolated land on the outskirts of a little hillbilly town called Hayfork in far Northern California. I mean, really? My brother came into this world in the exotic birthplace of the Buddha, and I was born in a log cabin in Hayfork? Something doesn't add up. I think I got cheated. Even my sister entered the world in the picturesque university town of Arcata. But hey, I guess Hayfork helped make me who I am today, for better or for worse. I've come to truly appreciate it in my adulthood, there are so many kind people there, but as a kid I felt like I was locked in a special type of hick hell. I didn't fit in.

When I was young I suffered from extreme anxiety and depression. As an adult, I still do, but I now understand what I'm going through and have some coping mechanisms in place. It's painful as a child to feel

Tiny me, naked in the hot springs.

anxious and miserable and not know why. With no clue how to fix the problem. You feel like that's what life is always going to be, so you try to distract yourself from your agony in any way possible, which only lasts for short spurts until the bad feelings come back.

Guarding my childhood home with my trusty cat, Buffy.

I remember experiencing such extreme worries about death that I could only feel happy when we had guests over to distract me from myself. It was a momentary reprieve I needed so badly. But then they would leave our house and that sick feeling in the pit of my stomach would come back. Sometimes it was literally a sick feeling in my stomach that hurt. I got terrible stomach aches from worrying so much. I'm honestly surprised I've never been diagnosed with an ulcer. It feels like I should have burned a hundred holes in my stomach lining by now.

I've looked back and assumed that all children experience the difficulties I endured with mental health as a young human being. I strongly suspect that many, far too many, do. But I've realized that there are a lot of kids who don't feel guilt and shame over every little thing. Maybe there are some kids out there who know how to be kids and enjoy carefree days while they have the opportunity. For me, the jury is still out on this topic. I think carefree childhoods are mostly a myth. I would like to have had one, but I doubt it's possible. Even today, my inner child is very jaded. And I think my inner child's inner child is *super* fucked up.

My dad with me, a friend, and our sweet dog, Sandy.

Chapter 29

Beloved Books

My favorite book is *The Secret Life of Bees* by Sue Monk Kidd. Incredibly captivating. Unexplainably intoxicating. The story rings in my heart like a cherished possession. I cling to those characters as if they were members of my own family.

The Narnia series by C.S. Lewis is a close second. They changed my childhood. My grandma Elisa and Uncle Anthony brought them to me one day when they visited us in Hayfork. Just before they became embroiled in an argument with my dad and stormed out of my life. I think Dad complained to them about something. Maybe showing up so late the night before. They never spoke to my father again. And I don't think that upset my father one bit. But the whole incident really hurt me. I was conflicted. Up to that point I was attached to my grandma. After that it was like she didn't exist to me anymore. I do love and admire her, but that event startled me so much I only fully reattached to her in adulthood. I'm sad I missed out on her for so many years.

Grandma Elisa has lived an extremely unique life as both a teacher and an artist, and when she was a young woman she spent a lot of summers in Mexico. On one of those trips she had a chance encounter with Frida Kahlo and Diego Rivera. Diego even kissed Grandma's hand. Swoon... what a story! It's like a work of art in and of itself.

I think of Grandma every time I pick up a Narnia book, and I so appreciate her introducing the series to me. Narnia is real in my mind. No questions asked. It's real. Because when I first read about it, I was young enough to become fully immersed. Consumed by its magic. If I were to choose which character I am out of the books it would be Lucy. Seems like the obvious choice, right?

And, speaking of Grandma Elisa, guess where she is right now? At the youthful age of ninety-one, my beautiful grandma is traveling through Italy and Greece with my amazing cousin, Devon. I am reminded of where my mother and sister inherited their world-traveling, adventurous side. Elisa is incredible. A worldly woman with an artist's eyes and a gypsy soul.

And speaking of adventurous women, *Eat, Pray, Love* is the most important book I've read in the last few years. When I first saw Elizabeth Gilbert's words on a page it changed the way I looked at my own writing. She was so conversational and honest. To me, a mesmerizing hero.

Literature can be unexpectedly impactful. I was once at a counseling appointment with a man who used a lot of EMDR during our sessions. For those of you who are unfamiliar with EMDR, it is a type of eye movement therapy that works to repattern the brain in such a way that it, in a sense, "erases" the pain of traumatic events. Something about the things I shared made him suggest I read the story of the Red Shoes in *Women Who Run With The Wolves*. That same day, after reading that passage, I worked up the courage to leave my first marriage. The odd thing about it is, I really don't remember much about the story now. And I just looked for my copy of the book, but can't find it. I would like to go back and reread it soon. It seems to me that the story was rather gruesome, like so many fables, fairy tales, myths and legends. But I know what I took from it was that I needed to be in charge of my own life. Never again was I going to give all my power away to someone other than myself. That story changed the trajectory of my life in the most curious ways. You never know when certain days will arrive, and you find that monumental change is just waiting to be unleashed, right below the surface, where it had been lurking all along. In the words of an author, in another human being who crosses your path, in a shattering defeat or a towering triumph. Change is change is change. Good or bad, it shakes things up. And to think that it often begins out of ideas gleaned from the pages of a little book.

Chapter 30

Me Giving Relationship Advice (Or, I'm Bad at Biting My Tongue)

When I have a friend or acquaintance going through a tough time in a marriage or long-term relationship, I feel compelled to tell them what I see from my perspective. I can't seem to hold back even if I know I should. It comes from a place of wanting to support the females in my life and remind them that they deserve uncomplicated love. And actually, I do the same when it's a male friend I'm supporting. People often just need a shoulder to lean on while they sort out their own feelings.

I had a friend once whose husband left her. She was crushed (as can be expected). The backstory was that her husband was a complete and utter sleazy schmuck. A selfish loser, in my opinion, and he didn't deserve her in the first place. I felt strongly about this even before there were signs of stress in their relationship. He was always putting her down in front of others, flirting too much with other people. And acting like he was God's gift to women because he was wealthy and drove a nice car.

So, do you have any ideas what I said to my friend when she broke down crying? I bet you know what I told her, right? Yep. I told her exactly how I felt about him, how I had always felt about him, and the fact that my feelings formed the second I was introduced to him. I told her I didn't trust him, worried he was unfaithful to her, didn't like his arrogance, thought his new sports car was stupid, hated the way he always talked down to her and exhibited such disrespect.

Don't get me wrong, I was a bit apologetic that I spewed all this negativity towards the man she loved, but I just felt she needed to hear it. She needed to hear someone tell her she deserved more. She deserved better.

Fast forward about a year later, and...*AWKWARD.* My friend's husband came crawling home to her and she let him back into her life. God knows why, but obviously it is not up to me who she chooses to love or be loved by. I just hope he learned his lesson and is treating her better. I have my doubts, but I love her dearly and to each their own. I will respect that she knows what's best for her.

In case you're wondering if this incident has changed my tendency to give unsolicited relationship advice, it hasn't. I know! I really do know!! I should have learned my lesson by now. But the last time I counseled someone whose husband was being a total jerk and, I think, having affairs left and right, I again shared how I felt with no filter. Except this time I made a point of apologizing in advance for my harsh words, and made sure she knew I wished them well (or at least I'll politely pretend to wish them well) if they ever choose to get back together.

It's so hard. We can see what we think other people should do in their relationships, but it's much harder when we are in the midst of a bad one ourselves. And even good relationships aren't meant to be perfect. Most are beautifully flawed in certain ways, but deep love is the glue that binds them together.

If you ever want overly blunt and direct, unfiltered relationship advice from me, all you have to do is ask! Heck, I'm even happy to give it if you *don't* ask. That is just the kind of giving, caring friend I am. And aren't you lucky to have me?

Chapter 31

He Didn't Believe in True Love

The relationship I was in before I met my fiance, Lefty, was weird. I'll call the guy David. He always said he didn't believe in true love. That should have been my first clue. I should have run the moment he confessed that nasty little bit of jaded pessimism. But of course I had to stick it out through horrible ups and downs for nearly four years. I cheated on him about a year in, which I am ashamed to admit, yet will reluctantly tell you about in a subsequent chapter. There are many reasons why it happened. I look back now and figure the main reason was because we weren't right for each other, but in the midst of a relationship disaster you never want to believe that it's really all hitting the fan because you're wrong for each other in every way.

David had an ex-wife from hell. Literally. I'm not even joking. She loved telling people that I broke up their marriage. I never could figure out how that was possible, because she was the one who left *him*. And by the time he and I were together they had been separated a good long while. Another favorite pastime of hers was to drive by me and yell and scream while flipping me off. She was simply a mean and bitter person. And there's so much more I could tell you. It only gets worse from there. But I'm going to do something uncharacteristic and not go into detail about the rest of her hellish behavior. Because something tells me she would like that. And I don't want to give her the satisfaction.

Yet, with all this said, I've tried over the years to send her less negative energy. None of us know what other people are going through. Yes, I admit I hated her with a passion back then, and she felt the same about me. But when you get distance from a terrible time in your life something called perspective happens. I've been able to understand that she would have hated anyone who dated her ex-husband, because she viewed people as possessions. I don't look at things that way. For anyone I loved in the past, I make an effort to wish them well. And to hope they find their own true love someday. Even if they swear they don't believe in it.

I loved this man, David, desperately and, throughout our years together, I forgot to love myself. And now that I actually know what true love is, because I have found it with Lefty, I'm amazed to find that I really never knew what it was before, either. Because I hadn't experienced it yet. Is placebo true love a thing? It sure seems to be. The tricky little devil.

I don't wish David any harm, in fact, on the contrary, I wish him happiness. But I look back at our time together and seriously wonder what on earth I was thinking. He once got mad at me for wanting to hang a pretty calendar on the wall of our bedroom with a thumbtack. He said the tack would damage his wall too much. Shouldn't that have been a sign that he wasn't mature enough to love me? He cared about the walls in the house more than he cared about me. It says it all right there. Couples who shouldn't be together are silly. So are the things they argue about instead of just dealing with the fact that they made a mistake getting together in the first place. Water under the untrue-love bridge, I guess.

I miss his parents. Well, not his mom. She was rather cold and snobby. You could feel a chill come through the air when she walked into the room. And I suppose I always held it against her that she basically abandoned David as a young boy. But I miss his dad and step-mom. They are wonderful people whom I still love dearly. And I also miss his daughters. I watched them grow up before my eyes while their dad and I were together, and then I had to sever ties when he left me. As if I meant nothing to them, and they meant nothing to me. But that was not the case. I can't speak for the way they felt about me. All I can say is that I loved them very, very dearly and I hope they never forget that. Sometimes I say hello to them in vivid dreams and I wake up crying. Dear girls, you are special and beautiful to me, and I wish you only happiness in this crazy journey we call life.

This topic has me thinking about the men I've fallen in love with over the years, and a strange realization is washing over me right now. It's occurring to me that the two "nicest guys" I've loved have actually hurt me the most. The guys who seemed like they were all heart and kindness. All warmth and caring. The person I'm speaking of alongside David is a high school classmate of mine named Mike. Mike was a year older than I and I fell hard for him when I was about seventeen. He made me believe he loved me. And yet, the last time I was supposed to see him with friends at the lake, he never showed up. Never called. Never explained. Nothing. I had to move on without saying goodbye or telling him what a jerk he was. It was just silence that lasted ten years. I say ten years because that was how long it took until we ran into each other again. At a friend's wedding. It was awkward. What we had between us all those years before was gone. We were practically two strangers exchanging the most superficial pleasantries. But it was good to finally feel a bit of closure.

So I guess that's it. That's my explanation about David and Mike. The two men I've ever had in my life that literally seemed like they couldn't hurt a fly and yet they hurt my heart in indescribably painful ways. And I think to myself, "Why did I trust them so much?" And I think, "Why was I so positive in those moments that they were the one for me?" And part of me answers my own questions: "Because you were stupid." But this may be a bit too harsh of an explanation. Honestly, I don't even know anymore.

What I do know, however, is that the memory of the day David broke up with me is seared in my brain forever. I wholeheartedly believed that we could get through anything. And I mean *anything.* I recall going to the river with my mom and my girls after he told me he was done with our relationship. A state of complete shock and denial took over my being. I'd never experienced rejection on this earth-shattering level before. I was weeping so profusely that it felt like I raised the sodium content in the water. I was utterly lost. Abandoned. Crushed. And for one of the first times since being born, I wasn't sure if I wanted to live anymore. What was the point?

Thankfully I was not truly suicidal, or else I would not have survived to heal. But heal I did. With strength and love to give to my new soulmate, Lefty. He is a huge reason why I was able to move on. I stare at him at times. Just in awe of his handsome face and the deep connection we have between our two souls. I would never go back to any day before I met him. I hope to never experience a day without him.

Last week I was reorganizing some pretty things on my bookshelf. One was a clear glass vase filled with shells, sea glass, and polished rocks. I poured out all my treasures onto a large plate so I could sort through and dust them off while deciding which ones to keep. Then I spotted it...a smooth heart-shaped rock in the center of the pile. I felt a little sick to my stomach. Immediately remembering how, when, and where this particular stone dropped into my life. Actually it dropped directly into the palm of my hand. David found it on the ground one day when we were hiking with all four of our girls. Our destination was some abandoned shooting range that gave me the creeps. As we were making our way back down the mountain, he bent down and picked up the rock and handed it to me.

At the time I thought it was sweet. But today, looking at that object I didn't know I still had, I realized something: The heart rock was black.

Jet black. Seeing it this time around, that seemed so fitting. A cold, stone black heart. Yep, that pretty much sums up the origin of our relationship troubles. I'm not saying David was some sort of a depraved monster, only that he seemed to have the capacity to worry about himself and sometimes his children, but no one else. His heart did not contain enough love to give me. And there is nothing I could have ever done to change that.

I decided to put the rock in my purse so the next time I'm outside, somewhere far from home, I can toss it off a cliff or into a flowing stream or waterfall. I don't want it anywhere near me. I don't need reminders of past experiences that killed pieces of my own beating heart. Times that almost stole my belief in love. I don't need to cling to the past which taught me so many things I never wanted to know. Here's to all the blessings of my bright reality and future. I feel so blessed to be in the here and now of my life's timeline. So very blessed indeed.

Chapter 32

Red Bulls and Vodka, Anyone?

I've never been a daily drinker. I go weeks, even months, without ingesting any form of alcohol. But there are times when I like to *drank!* I came to the conclusion a few years ago that maybe I'm a bit of a binge drinker. Because it used to be that once I started, especially in a social setting like a party or a bar, I wanted to keep going, and going, and going.

My favorite indulgence is whiskey. Perhaps because it takes me back to high school parties. Perhaps because I always have fun drinking it with my brother, who has the same affinity. I can assure you it's not the taste that's appealing. More like appalling. It's flat-out disgusting. And anyone who tells you otherwise is lying. But there's something about the way it makes me feel that hooked me a long time ago. It's like an old friend or a favorite pair of shoes. Comforting and familiar.

Here's the thing when it comes to whiskey, don't give me the top shelf bottle. In fact, keep that shit away from me, please. I want the straight-up Jack Daniels. I've had a love affair with Jack since the first time I met him. The effect is more energizing than sedating. You see, most alcohol makes me tired almost immediately. While Jack Daniels makes me feel sudden bursts of positive energy and creativity. It has always been my "happy place" drink.

There is such a variety when it comes to imbibing, and I always feel like I know a person that much better when they tell me their favorite drink. It's an interesting window into possible personality traits. I try not to judge people by what they're ordering at the saloon. To each their own, right?

But can I tell you something? I *hate* wine bars. First and foremost because I tend to dislike wine, but I think there's more to it. I feel like every wine bar I've ever been dragged to by a girlfriend, family member, or first date should have had a disclaimer posted in bold letters on the front door stating,

"ATTENTION: YOU ARE ABOUT TO ENTER THE MOST BORING, SNOBBY DRINKING ESTABLISHMENT IN THE CITY. COME ON IN! WE'LL JUDGE YOU FOR FREE, BUT YOU PAY FOR THE DRINKS."

I have a sincere aversion to people who think they are better than everyone else. And I'm sorry, reader, if you happen to be a wine drinker and I just spilled my Jack on the rocks all over your white carpet. I promise I know plenty of wonderful wine drinkers that don't fit the stereotype I'm describing. A few are dear friends of mine. So I know there are good ones out there. And recently I found out that Pink, the incredible singer we know and love, owns a vineyard and is making her own wine. I definitely would *not* have pegged her for a wine drinker. At all. So she is helping me shed some of the bad associations.

Beer used to immediately make me think of Homer Simpson. Frothy cold glass mugs of it in his fat, clumsy little hands. Nowadays I freely associate beer with Lefty. He's a Budweiser guy and he's adamant about it. He'll get bored once in a while and bring home Corona or Heineken, but that's a rarity. On the daily he's faithful to his red and white beer cans. And he sure is cute about it. People love to tease him about his love for such a standard beer (as opposed to specialty craft brews). It doesn't faze him. Just like the way I couldn't care less if people peg me for white trash when I drink Jack Daniels. That's okay! Maybe deep down that's exactly what I am. Except I'm extremely liberal. So...I don't know, would that make me blue trash?

The only time I ever blacked out from drinking was on a night I got together with one of my favorite girlfriends from high school. We were both around thirty years old, and she was passing through town to visit her mom, so we thought, "Let's go out, grab something at the bar and catch up!"

We walked around the corner to the nearest drinking establishment, pulled up a couple of them there bar stools, and waited for the bartender to tend to us. Meggan ordered a Red Bull and vodka and I thought that sounded intriguing, so I ordered one, too. It was a combo I had never tried and figured why not? The drinks came and I liked mine. It tasted good, so that was a plus. We were having a great time laughing and talking about our lives, our kids, our significant others, or lack thereof in my case. I guess this must have been during one of my momentary seconds in life when I wasn't involved with someone. Or at least not seriously. It had been a long time since Meggan and I had seen each other in person and we had so much ground to cover.

The drinks kept coming, we kept laughing too loud and shrugging off guys hitting on us. At some point we crossed the street to the only other bar in town.

Once we got to this second spot we were a solid five drinks in. And we were focused. We kept the Red Bulls and vodkas coming! I was having so much fun. More fun than I had had in awhile, actually. My life as a stressed out and broke single mom was not exactly a bundle of fun.

I woke up the next morning feeling absolutely awful. I was in my bed. I took a look at myself and all my clothes were still on. No jammies, no sign that I got ready for bed before I ended up there. My contacts were dry as hell and it hurt to open my eyes, so I was blinking profusely. That was another sign that I did nothing to prepare myself for bed. I can't stand sleeping in my contacts.

I thought about the night with Meggan. It was so great to see her! Then I thought long and hard about leaving the second saloon and the details of our walk home on the dark, quiet streets of Weaverville. The only trouble was that as much as I tried, I couldn't pull up a single memory of that part of the night. The last thing I remember I was sitting at the Diggins saying, "Sure, I'll have another!" And then there was just a complete time warp from that moment to the moment when I woke up with dry eyes and uncomfortable jeans.

What the actual fuck happened? I panicked a little bit. I took it as a good sign that at least I was waking up in my own bed and not someone else's. But still, how did I get home? Was Meggan okay?

I didn't spot her when I painfully got up and damn near crawled through the house, opening my eyes one at a time because my contacts were still driving me crazy. I didn't see any messages or texts on my phone from her either. Not even a note on the kitchen counter saying, "Hey drunk girl! I walked you home! You're welcome."

So I called her and confirmed that she had indeed been the one to see me safely to my doorstep. And she, too, got to her mom's safely on her own, thank goodness. I told her how shocked I was that the second half of the night was a dark patch of empty fog in my brain. That had *never* happened to me before. It scared the crap out of me!

I was so bothered by it I wanted to find out why it happened, and wondered if I was in danger of letting it happen again. I'm not always a complete control freak, but there's something kind of nice about ensuring you finish up an evening out while still having control of your conscious thought processes.

I came to this conclusion: Red Bulls, vodka and me don't mix. We had one date and after that I severed ties. Never again. Pretty damn sure the terrifying effect they had on me was that the caffeine allowed my body to turn off the, "I'm tired and I've had enough to drink" mechanism that normally clues me in when I need to cut myself off. It must have allowed me to order about six more drinks than I would have on any other occasion. I'm incredibly thankful for kick-ass girlfriends who know how to show you a good time *and* walk you home safely afterwards. Megs, you are a boss bitch and I love you!

Chapter 33

Buried at Sea

My mind often floats back to the last time I saw my sister. It's a recurring theme in my stream of consciousness and since I'm never going to make new memories with Naomi, I cling to my old ones for dear life. I had recently given birth to my first baby. Chloë was five weeks old when we arrived in Hawaii. We were picked up by dear family friends who were also visiting the island. I watched out the car window as whales breached the surface of the water. It seemed like they were signaling me. Telling me to soak up the joy on my trip, anywhere I could find it. But I wasn't feeling joy, I was feeling a terrible sense of dread. Bogged down by a sinking feeling in the pit of my stomach. A feeling that told me everything about life as I knew it was about to change.

We arrived in the town where my mom and sister lived. Mom had moved since the last time I saw her, into a little home attached to a beautiful Buddhist monastery. It had a meticulously manicured Japanese style garden in front. The picture of peace. Once the baby and I oriented to Mom's new spot and settled in to the extra bedroom, it was time to go see my sister.

The word radiant doesn't even go far enough to describe how stunning Naomi is in the photo above.

Naomi's place was a short distance across town. She rented a small but charming little house with an orange tree outside her bedroom window. As time wears on, I question my memory's reliability, but in my mind the house was painted a classic barn red. The color of rust or blood. Also like the hue of opium poppies. The kind that always grew in my hometown near the old art gallery.

I will never forget how beautiful Naomi looked when she opened her front door and stood there waiting for me to bring Chloë inside. She wore an oversized sweater. Her red curls wild on her head, blowing slightly in the breeze. Once inside she showed me around her place. It was so cute. She had it set up just the way she wanted it. All to herself. I quietly put my sleeping baby down and hugged Naomi. She was tiny. She had lost so much weight even since our last visit just a few months earlier. She seemed fragile. It was hard to see my usually strong sister like that. You could still see the strength in her eyes. Full of fire. But her body was betraying her at a rapid pace and I couldn't stand to witness it.

Naomi's leukemia had come back with a vengeance. An intruding relapse in a black cloak with no plans to leave alone. I still told myself she was going to fight it somehow. She just had to. I tried anything to stop myself from picturing her dying. That thought was an impossibility to me. I refused to believe it could really happen. But tragically, it *was* happening right before my eyes. And she knew it. She even told me she was worried about the grief her passing would cause. And she said she hoped we would all be okay.

This was strange to me. My sister was losing her battle to live and she was worried about *me*. As if it were her fault that she was being ripped away from us. I hated to think of her feeling guilty about an affliction she had no control over. Maybe her guilt originated from her choice to forgo that last round of chemo at UCSF. The last round the doctors so aggressively urged her to endure. But none of us have a crystal ball or a manual for the dos and don'ts of life. We simply have our gut feelings, our intuition, our hope that what we choose is right. She did her best. She felt the last round of chemo would kill her right then and there. Her body was so weak even though technically in remission, and she had a strong sense she would not make it through.

I used to dwell a lot on the "if onlies." If only Naomi had listened to her doctors at UCSF. If only she wasn't so stubborn. If only she had never become sick in the first place.

My sister on an adventure with a friend in Bangladesh.

But life doesn't operate on "if only." It operates on "it happened." And it did happen. The relapse took Naomi's life but it didn't take her spirit. I can still feel her around me sometimes. Still feel her love. Not as much as I wish I could, but I know we have an endless bond that will never go away. There are times when I can talk about her with people and feel alright about it. There are times when someone asks me if I have any siblings and I break down in tears. Even after eighteen years. The hurt remains. Losing her made everything a little *less.* Happiness is simply *less.* Never complete anymore. How could it be? My *heart* is not complete anymore.

I don't take even a minute of my time on Earth for granted. Naomi taught me that. Since I can't bring her back to life, I damn well better learn from her death. I have. And I continue to do so. I figure that's the best way to honor her existence and her memory. Every time my bare feet touch the ocean I think of her.

She was buried at sea. Like a sailor that didn't make it to the end of his journey. She got special permission from Hawaiian officials before she left her body. At first she was told no, but she pushed harder. She didn't want to be put into the ground, she didn't want fire to devour her either. What she wanted was to be wrapped in flowers and vines and released into the boundless sea. That's what Mom and her friends did for her. They took her body out on a sailboat, said their last goodbyes, and spread a layer of flowers on the surface of the water after they dropped her in.

Naomi lived her way and Naomi died her way. Fitting for a being as independent and unique as she was. I think she was too amazing for us to keep. She must have had somewhere else she needed to be.

Chapter 34

Wedding Plans

I never had a proper wedding the first time around. To be honest, I wasn't in any hurry to wed even after we found out we were having a baby, but as I've mentioned, Jason's mom (well meaning, opinionated, and loveable) kept insisting that the older members of the family would basically lose their minds if we brought a child into the world without being legally tied in a knot. I remember thinking, *Really? Are we living in the nineteen-fifties?* But I was young and prone to pressure and shaming, so there we found ourselves, eloping to the courthouse. Doing it our way.

Fast forward about seventeen years…

After a divorce, learning to be a single mom, entering the strange world of dating I'd never experienced before and a four year serious relationship that was mostly a serious waste of time, I'm now engaged to the man who I was looking for all along. I am ridiculously in love with Lefty, and we are PLANNING A WEDDING!

Today I got myself ready to be presentable in society during a one hundred and thirteen degree heat wave. I dragged my showered-but-already-sweaty-self out the door determined to start my window shopping for a wedding dress. I pulled up at the bridal shop feeling the tingle of excitement, and secretly hoping to find exactly what I was dreaming of on my very first try. I walked up to the door with my head held high, feeling like royalty approaching the gates of my new castle. I looked through the glass door at all the white dresses.

But, there was something wrong. The lights were off. That's when I spotted it: a sign on the door that said, "We will be closing at 2:45 p.m. today. Sorry for any inconvenience." All I can say is I hope the shop does not have security cameras with audio. And if they do, I pray they never have reason to review them, because I had some choice bad words rolling off my tongue into the hot summer air and onto their doorstep.

On a brighter note, this Monday Lefty and I are going to check out the possible wedding venue, and I'm very excited!

Update: I finally found my wedding dress a couple weeks ago!! Chloë and Gwen helped me. I tried on many hideous white garments before

I slipped into THE MOST AMAZING THING THAT HAS EVER SPARKLED ON THE FACE OF THIS EARTH. I cried, the girls cried, even the bridal boutique owner and her assistant cried. Real tears, not fake ones just to sell me more things. It was dreamy, surreal and thrilling.

Now for the other million things to do in order to prepare for our September wedding date...

Chapter 35

The Most Magical Day of My Life

"Close your eyes. Fall in love. Stay there."
– Rumi

The actual day was upon us. After countless hours of organizing, researching, agonizing and throwing money at everything under the sun (yet doing it all on a strict budget because neither one of us wanted to spend a fortune), we arrived at September 15th. I woke up buzzing with stress. Not about the idea of being legally wed to this incredible man who magically appeared in my life four years earlier, but simply about all the details of the day, and hoping and praying it would go alright, and that our guests would enjoy our special day with us.

Lefty and I didn't hire a wedding planner. We did it ourselves, with some amazing help from family and friends. If I realized just how many details would be involved, I may have broken down and looked into hiring someone to help us. But this was my first and only wedding, so I didn't really know what I was getting myself into. I'm glad. I really wouldn't

---

How did I get THIS lucky? If this is a dream, please don't wake me up.

have had it any other way. I get to be proud of what we pulled off. And when it was all tallied up, the cost was about ten-thousand dollars. A good chunk of money, but pennies compared to the amount the average American couple spends. Besides, we had not one, but two ceremonies. It started out with a traditional Lao ceremony, followed by traditional American nuptials, after a quick wardrobe change.

The best bridesmaids
I could've ever hoped for!

We arrived at our venue about half an hour later than planned. I think I stressed out the woman I hired to do hair and makeup. But she is a sweetie and was a good sport about it. I was lucky enough to have my daughters as my bridesmaids, so the makeup artist got busy right away. In the midst of this, I wasn't feeling the way I wanted to feel on my wedding day. I was a bundle of nerves, and kept worrying I would forget something important. And to top it off, I was *on my period*. Not just a little bleeding, but on the *heaviest day of my cycle*. Insane and stupidly unfair timing.

The girls and I got into our Lao traditional clothes. Special long skirts that wrap around, and for me, a brightly colored traditional top. The girls wore white tops, and we all had a special sash over our shoulder that fastened at the hip. A million double checks in the mirror later we were ready to start the first ceremony. I was in touch with Lefty by phone and we were biting our nails a bit because things were running late. We had to breathe, take a step back, and let the day take on a life of its own. Lefty and I were no longer in control, and we had to be ready to go with the flow. Um, no period pun intended.

Our smiles say it all.

Finally, the girls and I were told to come out

of the bridal quarters and gather on the traditional mat for the Lao ceremony. It was placed perfectly over the little dance floor at our venue. In the middle was the traditional centerpiece of Lao weddings and blessing ceremonies: a special silver creation holding an abundance of flowers and fruit with little white candles at the top. One of Lefty's uncles was there to officiate, dressed in a colorful turquoise Lao shirt and checkered sash.

Husband and wife expressing the ultimate respect for each other.

The second we all sat down to begin this ancient Lao tradition, I was overcome with emotion. For these ceremonies the candles are lit at the top of the centerpiece and the ceremonial chanting of the officiate begins. There are certain times we all lean forward and touch the centerpiece with both hands. Also, a plate of food is handed to both the bride and groom. This is held throughout the duration. Family and friends begin to come forth and choose a prayer bracelet to tie on the wrists of the man and woman getting married. As each individual ties them on, they give a blessing for a long, happy marriage. It is so personal, so intimate. With each person who tied a bracelet on my wrist, I could feel pure love pouring forth in abundance. I could sense centuries and generations of Laotian people practicing this beautiful tradition, and I was overwhelmed that I was able to be included in such a sacred practice.

I feel honored beyond words to be accepted into our Lao community. I often worry if I am saying or doing the right thing, but I am also aware that people are patient with me. I'm trying to learn what to do and what not to do. Especially around the Lao elders. The respect for elders is beautiful. It's exactly the way it should be. An awareness that each new generation that comes into being would not exist if it weren't for the hard work and sacrifice of the generations who came before. These elders have earned the reverence they receive from the younger members of the family.

Our traditional ceremony went on for quite some time, and the intensity did not wane one single bit. The blessings and bracelets and smiles and tears kept coming. It was an unexpectedly intense spiritual experience. I felt like the luckiest woman on earth, and I kept looking over at Lefty, next to me in his traditional clothing, in awe that this was the man I was marrying. His handsome, joyful qualities take my breath away. I never get tired of looking at his face, and I never take a single moment with him for granted. I know we are all just passing through this life, and I want every second I can have with him. I've never felt so genuinely loved by any other man ever. Blissed out does not come close to describing how I felt in the midst of this incredible traditional ceremony. It transported me across oceans, across lifetimes, across cultures. And it all felt deeply meaningful.

The time had come to go back to the bridal quarters and get into my white dress. The girls hurried into their bridesmaid dresses and then helped me lace and tie my corset back. My wedding shoes wouldn't buckle at first, and I started to freak out. But Gwen and her best friend Nhu saved the day and fastened them for me.

Pure joy!
(And me, looking like a blissed out idiot)

A few more glances in the mirror and we were ready to venture out and take our places, ready to walk down that aisle. My brother began to play the violin, and Gwen and my stepson, Cameron, walked first. Taking their places on the steps of the altar where Lefty and our wedding officiant, Rome, were waiting with anticipation. Next were Chloë, arm in arm with Lefty's endearing best friend, Mark. Then it was time. My dad and I linked arms and began the age-old tradition of the march to "give me away." Dad patted my hand lovingly as we began. It was so special to have this moment with him. And I felt like he was the proud father I always wanted him to be. A bonding experience like no other. And for a moment, time stood still and I just basked in the harmony of it all.

We got to the end of the rose petal aisle, and Dad walked me up the steps to meet Lefty. He stood there in his custom gray pinstripe suit. Patient, nervous, and gorgeous beyond description. Rome began to speak. Eloquent and heartfelt words that seemed to whisper of times gone by. A harkening back to the sacred beginning of life itself. Everything became a bit of an excited blur, and then it was time for the rings and to say "I do!" I'll never forget that kiss.

That was it. We were officially husband and wife. Ready to party with our guests and finally let down our hair for the rest of the night.

As a bonus, I sang a song for my new husband. One that I wrote just for the occasion, about a week earlier. My dad put guitar to it, and the two of us performed it together. The song is called *A Thousand Years or More* and the lyrics go like this:

I'll love you forever
But it won't be long enough
I'll love you in color
When memories fade to black and white
There ain't nothin you could do
To stop me from lovin' you

All I ask is for a thousand years or more
Hold me in those arms of yours
We can weather any storm
Long as we keep each other warm
All I ask is for a thousand years or more

I loved you the first time
That I ever saw your face
And I'll love you the last time
That we can embrace
There ain't nothin' you could do
To stop me from lovin' you

All I ask is for a thousand years or more
Hold me in those arms of yours
We can weather any storm
Long as we keep each other warm
All I ask is for a thousand years or more

Along the way we might drive each other
Crazy sometimes
But that's okay, true love don't promise
That every day will shine

But I'll love you forever
And it won't be long enough
And I'll love you in color
When memories fade to black and white
There ain't nothin you could do
To stop me from lovin' you

All I ask is for a thousand years or more
Hold me in those arms of yours
We can weather any storm
Long as we keep each other warm
All I ask is for a thousand years or more

Mmmmm
A thousand years or more
Mmmmm
All I ask is for a thousand years or more

And with that, our wedding experience was complete. Laughter, tears, pictures, pictures, pictures and most of all, happiness. The only thing I wish is that the day had lasted longer. By the time I shed my nervous energy and was having a fabulous, carefree time, it was over. Just like that. Short, sweet, and amazing. One for the history books, folks.

Chapter 36

It's Art, for God's Sake

My sandblasted mirror was turning out to my liking. It was a simple rendition of my favorite angel picture from the Sistine Chapel. Two chubby angels daydreaming. I was feeling proud of my work when my art teacher came over to look at it. He told me I'd better use a second sand blasting technique before I finished it up. One technique wasn't enough.

This may sound silly, but his words infuriated me. I was accustomed to being immersed in various styles of art my whole childhood. Pencil drawing was my favorite and I was actually pretty darn good at it. I loved to paint as well. But I hated to be told how to do my art. I always thought to myself, *It's ART for God's sake, does it have to have rigid rules, too?* Can't anything in life just be free-flowing and creative without confinement? My stubborn nature does not mix well with being told what to do. Especially in an area I am passionate about. In fact it's one reason why I never majored in art or music in college. I knew that making those things mandatory would jeopardize my deep dedication to both fields.

I feel strongly that our American school system is too hung up on forcing kids to do things they don't want to do. Or forcing them to forgo doing projects their way. They are told they are wrong if they don't do things like everybody else. But just think how many great feats have been accomplished by those who dare to jump off the cliff of conventional society and into the sea of infinite possibility. That's where I want to be. Floating in the salt water of creation and intrigue. Manifesting that which they say cannot exist.

I'm pretty sure I never did augment that mirror project of mine. I settled for a lower grade because I knew the lower grade would bug me far less than altering my precious looking glass. It was what it was, and it was exactly what I wanted it to be. My art teacher was a wonderful person, and he was just doing his job, and even though I can take a step back in my mind and understand that he had strict criteria for grading our work,

I still can't condone the system that made him have to operate that way. We are educating the creativity *out of America's children*. And for that we should all be ashamed.

One of my favorite ways to use my art skills during my teens had nothing to do with school. I joined a summer mural painting project through a local job training organization. The best part about it was that I got to work with my private art teacher, with whom I had taken lessons for years. She is a legend in Trinity County. Bella Peralta. A beautiful, fun-loving, artistic genius who came to America from England in her younger years. Her family members were the official weavers for the royal family. I mean, how awesome is *that?!* Bella is art royalty of the most honorable kind.

The mural we painted was at the public pool in Weaverville. It was a scene with a sandy beach and a jungle, with an ancient palace off in the distance. The part I painted that I'm most proud of is a life-size tiger. Stretching up and resting his huge paws on a stone column. That tiger was my baby during this particular summer. I nurtured him and brought his stripes to life in the hot sun. And I've prepared ever since for the day I hear the mural was painted over, or the wall knocked down. That's what happens to most local art pieces eventually. People who are not artists see the need for change and demolish others' creations. It's sad. I have photos to remember the mural by when that day comes. And I hope when it does, my beloved tiger will understand.

Chapter 37

Pretty Sure John Prine Is the Father of Jesus

People always ask me, when they learn I'm a singer, "What do you sing? Who are your influences? Genres! We need to know about your preferred genres!!!" These issues are hard to address, because I like to sing and write within almost every genre under the sun. And I have too many favorite singers to name or count.

But something I do have is a favorite song. "Angel from Montgomery." Written by the great John Prine. I love the versions by Bonnie Raitt and Susan Tedeschi equally. And when I get to stand up on a stage, big or small, and sing that song with all my heart, I am complete.

As a songwriter, I'm constantly trying to dissect what it is that's so wonderful about iconic songs. Something about the way the lyrics and melodies transport us into another realm. Songs that, when heard for the first time, make us aware we are no longer the same person we were before our ears were filled with this new, mystifying magic. And we are never going back to the way we were again. Forever changed. Forever a little bit better than before.

Great songs are enchanting creations that can entertain, uplift, and sometimes expose us to new ways of thinking. They can also allow us to cry it out. All the tears. Let 'em drop onto the barroom floor. And slip between the cracks of the floorboards that have seen too much. Music is the great evoker of emotion. And no soul is immune from its effects.

How unique can you get, John Prine? Starting your masterpiece of a tune out with the words:

"I am an old woman
Named after my mother
My old man is another
Child who's grown old
If dreams were thunder
Lightning was desire.
This old house would've burned down
A long time ago..."

Just typing these lyrics and I'm getting the chills. Words have power. Songs like this are medicinal. The only drug I'll ever need. It's intoxicating, the journeys people can take us on. Floating on the wind of their words, we're allowed to borrow the wings of their melody and look at the world from a vantage point that's upside down. But perfectly meant to be that way.

I've always wanted to write a song about whiskey. I don't know, it just seems like you're not *really* a singer-songwriter until you've written your whiskey ballad. So I was pretty excited to wake up the other morning to a song writing itself in my head. A song about the gross-tasting brown liquid I love so much. It's called, "Whiskey Kind of Morning," and it's from the perspective of an unhappy woman trying to drink away her tears. Tears caused by an unfaithful man in her life. She's trying to cover up her sorrow with Jack on the rocks, but she's also trying to utilize the alcohol to be brave enough to leave him. In this song, whiskey becomes both the poison and the cure.

The funny thing about writing songs like this is that people will often say to me, "But I thought you were happy with your new husband! What happened?!" Um...nothing happened. Lefty is amazing and I am blissfully in love with him. And guess what? I have an imagination that allows me to write from any perspective about real and unreal events anytime I want. And I love it. Once we've experienced great love, great loss, heartache, betrayal, disappointment in ourselves, we can conjure up any of those feelings at the drop of a hat and set them to music. Actors don't have to personally experience the content they are acting out in order to be believable. And I don't have to be miserable to write a break up song. Break up songs are the *best.*

Update: I was devastated to learn recently that John Prine passed away. Noooooooooooooo! Such a sad loss. I feel for his family, friends, and the entire music industry. So tragic and disappointing.

Chapter 38

Never in a Million Years Could I Have Seen This Coming

I always had mixed feelings about my Grandpa Herman. Something told me to keep my distance. I got the sense that he might act inappropriately with me if I wasn't careful around him. I'm proud of the Polish heritage he passed on to me, and his poetry, but that is where my admiration stops. He spent his life as one of the most unique individuals to walk this planet. Abandoning my mom and her brother when they were three and five, he ran off to womanize, write, and drink as he pleased to his heart's content. He started the National Poetry Association, based in San Francisco. Maya Angelou once spoke to praise him at a lifetime achievement award gala. I wanted to meet her so badly. But she left before I could beg someone to introduce me. She and I shared a birthday, and I have always worn that fact as a bright shiny badge of honor. I want so much for that to mean I might have even five percent of the power in my words that she did in hers. I'd happily settle for five percent and be proud.

When my grandpa passed away at ninety-five years old, it began the unraveling of that side of the family. And there aren't many of us to unravel. It comes down to my Aunt April. A person incredibly important to me my whole life. A woman who, when my sister died, became the closest thing I had to a sister in her place. A figure to help fill that endless void, even if just a little. But the painful thing is that it wasn't just a little, it was a lot. April meant so damn much to me and I always felt that I meant a heck of a lot to her, too.

Aunty April is Mom's half sister. Nineteen years younger than my mom and thirteen years older than I. When Grandpa Herman abandoned my mother and her brother, he lived many years as a free-wheeling poet with no responsibilities. Then he shacked up with a young woman twenty-five years his junior. Their love child was named after the season of sunshine and flowers and spring showers. Though she was not born in April but in January. January second, to be exact. I'm afraid Aunt April did not have it easy growing up, because even though her father actually stuck around to raise her, she ended up raising him instead. He didn't know how to care for anyone but himself. Yet, he did treat her as some sort of golden child, and seemed to beam whenever she was around. It was not her fault, but it would make me angry how much he doted on her compared to my mom. It was like Herman started his life over and it didn't include Mom and her brother, Konstantine, ever again.

As Herman neared the end of his life he became somewhat senile. I say somewhat because it seems that it was less severe than what his siblings endured towards the end of theirs, but it was still pretty bad. He started calling my mom his "girlfriend" when she took care of him. I hope it was purely out of confusion from the dementia, but you could never really tell with him. I honestly don't know how my mom was able to care for him so selflessly. She is a much better person than I am.

Upon Herman's death my mom and April were asked to attend a meeting about his estate. In this meeting, Mom found out a harsh reality. Turns out that she would not inherit half of Herman's property in the old seaside hippie town of Bolinas, California. The property she had always loved. It was nothing fancy, but had a big place in her heart, and because of its location, had quite a hefty price tag as well. Half would not go to my mother because April's mom, Sophia, had passed away a couple years earlier. She had a detailed will that split the property in half instead of having it converted to grandpa's name in full. Sophia's half was willed solely to Aunt April. And April had two years where she sat on this knowledge that would impact my mom so greatly. She had two full years where she could have had the uncomfortable discussion with Mom and told her what Sophia's will said about what would go to whom in the end.

I should note that Sophia and Herman had been separated for at least thirty or forty years but never legally divorced. This meant their finances were still enmeshed but their lives were lived separately. Sophia in a high rise apartment in the heart of San Francisco, Herman in a tiny shack in Bolinas, across the fence from a sizable rental house that brought in income for both of them. My grandpa was a simple man and didn't seem to mind having very little. As long as he had bottles of wine, and was allowed to smoke his pot, he was as happy as an old Polish poet could be. The one thing I loved about him was that he hummed classical music almost twenty-four seven. And he did it with *gusto!* Such a passion for music. It was beautiful to witness. I'm glad that the last time I saw him alive I was able to tell him how much I had always enjoyed his love of classical arrangements. He passed that love on to me, and for that I am thankful.

As Mom and April proceeded to make sense of this messy inheritance business, the gravity of everything hit me like a hurricane midway through a sunny day in July. The confusion and grief came fast and it came hard. You see, Herman didn't have a will. Or at least there was never one found. This meant that his half of the property and everything on it was split between his two daughters. How it would end up is that April was entitled to three quarters of the land, and my mom was entitled to one quarter. I can only imagine how forgotten my mom must have felt when this all started to sink in. Her dad chose to forget about her when she was a little girl. Then he forgot about her again when it came to ensuring any equality between her and her sister after he was gone.

To be clear, I wouldn't even be writing this passage if my aunt had decided to be fair and split the property in half with my mom. I can promise that's what my mom would have done for her if things were turned around. She could have easily disregarded her mother's will. As in, "Thanks, Mom, I appreciate you were looking out for me, but I'm okay with splitting our dad's portion of the inheritance with my sister." It would have allowed us to stay intact as a family with the aunt I was so attached to. I've tried over and over and over again to to see things from her point of view. I've had many honest conversations with myself (not around others, they might peg me for a crazy) to assess whether I'm selfishly just mad about the money my mom and I will miss out on because of this uneven property split. I've tried to dissect my feelings and look at the situation from every possible angle. But I just can't seem to let my aunt off the hook. She received hundreds of thousands of dollars from her mom. Then she decided she was also entitled to take more than her fair share of their dad's place.

Here's where I will acknowledge and admit that I am obviously not very evolved. People say that forgiveness is the answer. Forgive and forget. But I can't seem to forgive or forget. I wish my aunt well, but I recently did the petty thing and unfriended her on Facebook. It was too painful to see her face come across my screen. The face that had brought me so much joy as a child when she would visit. The face that signaled to me that I was deeply valued and cared for by her. I'm probably repeating myself, but she was *so important* to me my entire life. More so than I can accurately explain here. How do people go from that kind of bond to feeling sick to their stomach when they see each other come across social media feeds?

Before it got to this point, I tried to find a way to work through all this and keep my aunt in my life in a healthy way. I sent her a couple messages laying my bleeding heart on the floor. Told her exactly how I felt, and why I was so confused and thrown off by her seemingly selfish actions. I told her that I felt like she chose money over family and I thought her love for me was more unconditional than that. I'm sure it stung her to hear my angry words, but I also made it clear I still loved her and needed her in my life. People are funny. Some are comfortable with saying everything on their mind when they're upset and hurt, others are only comfortable to skim the surface of their emotions and hope the rest that lingers underneath will disappear before they have the awkward task of experiencing them, or worse, sharing them with others. I learned through all this that my aunt is a "skim the surface" kind of girl. There's a quote by Maya Angelou that goes like this: "When people show you who they are, believe them the first time." Well, I'm trying to believe my aunt about who she is and stop missing who I always thought she was. I haven't succeeded yet. I miss her dearly. But I guess we'll both survive.

Update: As if taken straight out of a soap opera script, it turns out that just recently a will *was* found from my grandfather. It was written many years ago. Here's the bombshell of it all: It leaves the entire Bolinas property and dwellings to April, and a bit of money to my mom. So, Mom will end up getting about one hundred and forty thousand dollars and my aunt will walk away with one point eight million when she sells the place.

I don't know what my grandfather was thinking when he wrote this. I've never been impressed with his "parenting skills" or maturity level. But all I could think when I heard about it was how heartbreaking it must be for Mom. Like being abandoned all over again. And yet my aunt still has a choice. She could choose to make it right, but instead I know that she is choosing to roll in her money the way a freshly washed puppy likes to roll in cow patties or horse manure. I can picture her finding glee in getting the fresh money scent all over her pale skin.

I know Aunty April chose to take it all because I have already received the manila envelope from her lawyer confirming as much, in nauseatingly stale legal mumbo jumbo. It might as well have said: "To whom it may concern - April Berlandt has acknowledged that she did indeed inherit every selfish gene that both her parents so generously passed down to her, and now she's taking the entire property, as well, because that's what selfish people do."

Have fun with your money, Aunty April. I hope it loves you unconditionally the way I did for far too long.

And now I must put all this anger and immaturity away for a while, before it eats me alive. I know it's not pretty or kind or becoming of one who prides herself on trying hard to lend compassion to others. I'm sorry if I got carried away, but this shit is *hard.* I keep trying to figure out what I can learn from this whole sickening mess. And all that comes to mind is that I've learned who I don't want to be. I don't want to be like the younger half sister or the sibling-like aunt who wakes up one morning with only riches on her mind. Selling her shallow soul to the money gods and turning her back on the ones who used to be the closest to her heart.

Chapter 39

I Don't Like Wearing Aprons

I like to make grilled cheese sandwiches. I like to make quesadillas. And, full disclosure, what I like better than making them is eating them. Turns out I melt cheese on bread and tortillas very well. But it stresses me out to follow recipes. I reserve that kind of cooking for special occasions. I must say, though, I make some darn good spaghetti and garlic bread. That's one thing everyone in my family seems to agree on. The trick is lots and lots of onion, garlic, and veggies in the sauce that simmers for hours. My other favorite go-to meal is homemade egg rolls. They are amazing. Probably the one thing I make that I am always one hundred percent proud of. Bring on the hot mustard and sweet and sour sauce! NOW!

Most of the time, cooking and cleaning are hard to get excited about. I used to think something was wrong with me. I'm a woman, yet it's an extreme struggle to want to make dinner, do laundry, clean the bathrooms. Somehow I thought it would come more naturally. But that theory is bullshit. Women are often no more suited for household chores than men. And actually, I know a lot of men way better at it than I am.

That's okay. I'd rather be writing, singing, songwriting, performing, painting, making love, skinny dipping in the South Fork of the Trinity River. I'd rather do just about anything than be a housewife. Being a wife in the right marriage: great! But the term "housewife" makes me want to throw up. To my wonderful man's credit, though, I genuinely enjoy taking care of him as much as I can. And in return, he takes care of me, too. Isn't that the way it's supposed to be?

Fun Fact: I'm watching TV as I finish this section of the book, and an interview with Amy Sedaris just came on. Her spoof on a domestic home show is *priceless*. Now *she* is a housewife I can relate to! Bring on the donut bird feeders!! Because, in Amy's words: "If there's one thing I know about birds it's that BIRDS. LOVE. DONUTS." Amen to that, Amy. A-fucking-men to *that*.

Chapter 40

Guest on the Mountain

I was eight and she was six. Mikaela and I met in a homeschooling group and somehow recognized we were kindred spirits. We both had unusual upbringings, lived in remote cabins in the woods, and longed for some sort of mainstream "normalcy." Looking back now, I believe we are both very thankful for the way we were raised, but when we were kids it seems like we had a lot of hard growing pains. Trying to find ourselves amidst the forests and the salamanders in our backyards.

I envied the way Mikaela's family doted on her. She was an only child brought up by not two, but three parents. Her mom and dad found land on the side of a mountain that you couldn't even drive to. You had to park in a small gravel area, then hike a quarter mile straight up a well worn path. When Mikaela's parents settled on their land, they brought along her father's best friend, Joe. Shortly after Mikaela was born, her mom and dad (Randi and Jim) parted ways in terms of romance, but they all continued to live on that mountain, raising the cute little Mikaela with rosy cheeks and pretty freckles.

Over time the three parents built three picture-perfect little cabins. None of them within visual distance of the others. I felt like a lucky fairy in fairyland whenever I got to be the guest of honor at "The Land," the endearing nickname of their mountain home. I can easily say that most of my best childhood memories come from those weeks with this amazing family. Mikaela and I loved to play pretend games and run around in the woods. Sometimes we built small sand swimming pools for her pet rat to test out her aquatic skills. I could never quite tell whether this was fun for the cute pet, or if we were tormenting her. But it was fascinating to watch her dog paddle around in the water. The rat had a cage in Mikaela and Randi's cabin but was not required to stay in it. It was more like an optional place to hang her little hat. Most of the time she ran around the house like a small extra child. Finding tiny items to hide for a rainy day behind her inclosure.

Randi was (and still is) such an incredible mother. Deeply caring and fun. A completely beautiful soul, inside and out. One of my favorite things she did for us was reading aloud while Mikaela and I played or did craft projects. And we often went on trips to the Humboldt coast to frolic in the cold waves and search for agates on the beach.

Randi has endured cancer three times. Three separate types of the disease. She is a strong survivor who inspires everyone who is lucky enough to know her. A writer, singer, songwriter, and botanist, she is creative and broad minded. Hanging out with her makes me feel grounded, loved, and fully alive.

Mikaela has grown up to become an incredible creative force herself. Mind-blowing talent oozes out of her pores. She is a clothing, jewelry, and costume designer. Currently living in Los Vegas. I love keeping up with her grand adventures by way of social media. We rarely see each other in person anymore. But the love is still there. Right where it should be. Right where it will always be.

Her fathers are two of my favorite men on earth. Very different from one another. I think Mikaela lucked out because whatever she didn't get from one in the way of parenting, she would get from the other. And vice versa. One funny memory I have of Jim and Joe was when they took Mikaela and me camping. I don't remember the trip much except for this one snippet: Mikaela had to go to the bathroom and Joe was instructing her to conserve toilet paper by only using two or three squares at a time. Then Jim came over, after hearing Joe's careful lesson, and handed Mikaela an extra roll of TP and said something to the effect of, "Okay sweetie, and when you're done doing it the way Joe instructed, here's more paper to do it right." I still laugh thinking back to that moment. It's really the perfect illustration of Jim and Joe. Two totally different, totally wonderful fathers.

Sometimes Mikaela, Randi, and I slept indoors when I came to stay, and other times we slept outside in a tent in their field near the garden, or way up high in a huge water tower I got stuck in every time. I could go *up* the straight up and down ladder, but coming down was a different story. I would freeze like a petrified wild animal approached by a human for the first time. I don't think I used to recognize what a strong fear of heights I had.

I don't miss inching my way down that ladder, but I do miss sleeping under the stars in that tower with Randi and Mikaela. Girl time was insanely fun with those two. We giggled about anything and everything, and whenever we were together I felt safe. It was like I was right where I was supposed to be. I loved my own family, but whenever I was in my own home my gnawing depression and anxiety would find me and there was little to nothing I could do to escape it. But when I was up on The Land, I was free. It had this magical power to liberate me from my demons that kept me up at night. It was my happy place. And as with many of my favorite memories from childhood, I feel an unexplainable sadness whenever I think of it. I think it comes from a mix of missing it all so deeply and the fact that I know I can never go back.

Of course, physically I can arrange to venture up that mountain again someday to see our old stomping grounds, but it will never be the same. That's the thing about life, we have moments in time that disappear, and once they pass, that's it. They're over and they'll never be duplicated. They were a one-shot deal. I'm just so happy I got to experience them when I did.

I credit this beautiful family with so much of who I have become in my life. They taught me about what is important and how to be strong. I love all four of these human beings fiercely and without condition or end.

Chapter 41

I Knew

I've been spending a weird amount of time wondering where I got this despair complex that follows me around most days like an unwanted friend. Then, BAM! It hit me like a ton of bricks a couple days ago. The reason I am so afraid of being persistently positive, laser focused on success and the goodness of life, is because I clung to that type of positivity with my entire being when my sister was sick. In my mind I KNEW Naomi was going to survive. I KNEW everything was going to work out in her favor. I just *KNEW*. I even promised her she would make it through. I literally said those words during one of the last phone conversations we were afforded. I believed vehemently that she was meant to survive. And when she died I shut down. And stopped believing I was capable of truly knowing anything ever again. I was angry with God. I was angry with every person who told me Naomi was in a better place. That felt like a line meant more to comfort the person uttering it. But it did not comfort me.

I take my promises seriously. The words "I promise" don't come out of my mouth often. And I feel a sense of guilt and shame that I dared to promise my sister she would beat the cancer coursing through her veins. Through the marrow of her bones.

I wish I had been allowed to keep that promise.

Chapter 42

Work

When I'm at my desk at the college where i work, I'm aware that every hour that goes by, I'm a little less alive. I don't know why. Why it drains me the way it does. It's like an energy vacuum sucking my vitality away one email at a time. There's something wrong with the flow of things here. Like what really matters doesn't matter. And what doesn't matter is, in this environment, *everything.*

I get confused because I love a lot of the people I work with, and most of the students I serve as well. So why is it such a trial to get through each day? I think it's partly because my strengths are not strengths in this setting. They are not valued by the organization. And even though I love the organization, our differences make it hard. My strengths are kindness, compassion, empathy. My strengths are listening and understanding people when they need a shoulder to lean on. But the college doesn't want these strengths. They want me to be more of a business person, make better excel spreadsheets, checklists, flow charts. Fuck flow charts. I can't do it. I'm capable, but I refuse to reduce my life down to some silly organizational pattern on a piece of paper. It means absolutely nothing to me, and I can't even pretend otherwise.

I got in this morning to all the things left on my to-do list from yesterday. I wanted to scream when I glanced at it, because I already had five more things added to my urgent tasks by my boss, and there simply aren't enough hours in my day. This secretarial position is practically designed to make someone feel like a failure during their drive home every night. Never one hundred percent done, always loose ends that will never be tied up tight. Never. Because that's not the nature of the job. It's this big fucking never ending circle that, just when you think you've reached a completion point, starts all over again. I don't have the patience. And I don't know if I should be ashamed about this or not. Because here's the truth of the matter: I don't even *want* to have the patience.

I stay up late worrying about how I will ever extricate myself from this narrow box. A terribly miss labeled box. It's marked "Low Level

Secretary" when what I really want it to say is "Grammy Winning Singer," "Best Selling Author," "Songwriter of the Year."

I've fallen down on the job of life lately. I've betrayed myself and stolen too many years from me along the way. For that I am sorry, because I can see the anguish it's caused written all over my face in the restroom mirror each time I take a bathroom break. I look empty and hollow. Completely incomplete. Sad eyes full of disappointment stare back at me and I have to look away before my emotions become too strong to return to my workstation and pretend everything is fine.

I didn't think I would be in this predicament. Not at this point in my life. I thought by now I would have found my way. I thought by now I would have conquered my roadblocks and fears. Where is my inner strength I always thought I possessed? It has forsaken me for supposed financial security. But how financially secure can I really be while bringing home a whopping twenty-thousand dollars a year? Thank God Lefty is so supportive. I wouldn't be able to support myself and my girls on my own. Not with my current position. It's only twenty eight hours per week with the added bonus of feeling like sixty. And I don't get child support from my ex-husband, either, even though I am the sole custodial parent. So, yay for that extra little gem. But that part is my own fault for never pushing for it. I just didn't have it in me to get into a big money battle with my ex.

Jaded qualities ooze out of my pores. I try to contain my disdain for conventional lifestyles, but I don't think I do a very good job. It would make it easier if I could appear to be okay with things I'm not okay with, but that's not who I am. And it's not who I will ever be.

Speaking of that, this crazy thing used to occur around twelve noon on workdays. Someone would plan an impromptu birthday party or congratulatory celebration for one of my co-workers and suddenly everyone would clear out of the office and jovially head out to a restaurant for a group lunch. Now, I bet you're thinking to yourself, "That doesn't sound crazy. That's normal workplace behavior." But here's the crazy part: I was the one person in my area of the office who never got to go. Sure, I know I was part-time, but that was beside the point. No one ever bothered to say, "Hey Arianna, why don't you join the party this time, I'll stay back and watch the desk." Just once in a while would have made all the difference for me. I feel stupid that I broke down crying about my hurt feelings to more than one co-worker on more than one occasion. The act of always being the one left out made me feel like a little girl no one wanted to play with. Or the one always picked last for a sports team at school. That's a really, really crappy feeling. And it took a long time for my office to stop doing it and decide to have more potlucks at the back table or order in from a local eating establishment.

I am telling this story to illustrate the differences in people. Some don't think twice about a situation, as long as the chips are stacked in their favor. While others are the ones who say to their co-worker, "You need to take a break. Go ahead and have fun. I'll cover this time, and next time we can switch." Fairness is not rocket science, it just takes a level of consciousness that holds it up as a top value. When that's the case, it's easy.

I know I sound like such a baby blah-blahing about being left out of office parties, but those experiences are what cause deep unhappiness in work environments. When you have to be the one to stand up and say to someone, or a group, "Hey, I'm here, too. And I matter." That means there is already a systemic problem in office dynamics. And it didn't just start when you were hired on.

People at work seem to take policies and procedures so seriously. And me? Well, I diligently try to follow the rules and work hard. I have a good work ethic. I'm not a flake or a slacker. I promise I'm not. But I can't buy into everything I'm supposed to do, hook line and sinker. I can't. I won't. I'm supposed to be alright with always getting the short end of the deal and I'm not alright with it. Taking home pay that keeps me below the poverty line yet working five days a week and commuting too far to boot. It's a special kind of insanity.

The moments that bring me happiness at work are when I get to visit with the students and find out how things are going for them. I love discussing their classes, and cheering them up when they've gotten a bad test score and feel like they can't keep going. I remind myself that this is why I'm in this position. But I don't know how much longer I can handle it. Something is killing me here, and I hope I don't stick around long enough to find out if I'm right.

Chapter 43

Makeup

I've always had fun with makeup, but I've never been that woman who does it flawlessly and has every hair in place 24/7. I don't even understand women like that. Part of me envies them, and another part of me feels freaked out by them. Sometimes when girls walk around looking overly perfect every second, I have this strong urge to go up to them and say, "Honey, what's *really* going on with you? Like, on the inside?"

Blush is a confusing subject. Do I put it on in diagonal lines across my cheeks? Do I use it in circles on the "apples" of my cheeks? Do I use it in wide swaths and then blend it in? I don't know. I feel like I get it right about fifty percent of the time. The other fifty percent I walk around looking like a friendly clown. I'm learning from YouTube videos. And I think I'm getting a little better. Next time you see me out and about, please let me know if I look like I should be wearing oversized shoes, holding a gaggle of balloons and squirting people in the eye with fake flowers. If so, I assure you it will be right back to the blush tutorials for this girl.

My favorite lipstick color is pink. I own at least ten shades of pink lipstick, but only use one or two on a regular basis. The shade has to be perfectly pastel and not overly shimmery. I currently love "Snob" by Macy's MAC collection. I usually use cheap, cheap lipstick, so I don't really like paying seventeen dollars for a new tube, but it's worth it. I don't like the name, but I do love the color.

Chapter 44

Seized with Fear

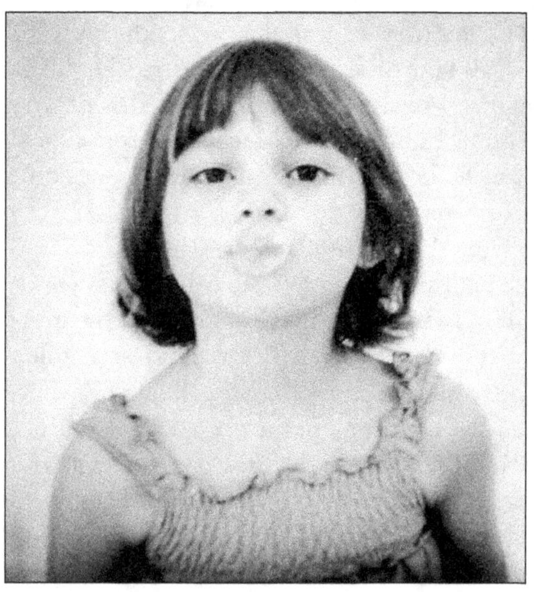

Gwen called me into the bedroom. I had just tucked her and Chloë in fifteen minutes earlier. When I opened the door Gwen said, "I think Chloë's throwing up!" I heard it too; it sounded like choking or gagging. I flicked on the light and looked at the top bunk. Chloë was flat on her back but seemed to be having a hard time breathing. I jumped up on the ladder to reach her and turned her over on her side. Trying to talk to her, I realized to my horror that she was unresponsive, staring wide-eyed into space. Turning her body did make her stop sputtering, but I was panicking. I kept saying her name loudly. Over and over. And this terrible-beyond-words feeling grabbed ahold of me. Was my daughter dying? I honestly thought for a second she was gone. It was the scariest moment of my entire life. Shock and despair rolled into one. And her sister was panicking with me. She kept asking me if Chloë was okay. I could

---

Little Chloë the cutie pie! Photo: Jil Chipman.

tell she was just as afraid as I was that we were losing her. It was painful to try to reassure Gwen that her sis would be alright, when I myself was seriously petrified that she was slipping away right before my eyes.

Suddenly, Chloë's big eyes rolled back into her head. I finally understood. She was having a seizure. I had already asked my boyfriend, David, to call 911, and I knew they were on their way. But this was Trinity County. Ambulance arrivals take time to navigate the treacherous mountain roads. Waiting was agony. I reassured Gwen again. This time slightly relieved because at least now I knew why Chloë was unconscious. And, though I was still scared as hell, I began to have hope that she could hang in there until the EMTs arrived.

An eternity later, the EMTs did arrive. They rushed into the house, put an oxygen mask on my girl, and tried to calm me down. Once the oxygen started kicking in, I saw Chloë move slightly for the first time. She kind of half turned her body, and my relief was indescribable.

She was loaded into the ambulance. Then came a heart wrenching moment. There was only room for me to go with Chloë. Gwen would have to stay back with David. She was already panicked and traumatized, now I had to tell her she couldn't have the comfort of being close to me while we took her sister to the hospital.

My boyfriend picked Gwen up and cuddled her while I told her I loved her so much. I told her my mom would be there soon to pick her up and bring her to me. It wouldn't be long. Chloë and I left in the ambulance. She was still out of it, but beginning to come around a bit. We arrived about an hour later at Mercy Hospital in Redding. After she was checked in, they whisked her away for a brain scan.

I wasn't too worried at this point. Chloë was a happy, healthy twelve year old. I doubted anything was truly wrong with her brain. And I knew that once in a while people had seizures for no apparent reason. It was unsettling, but not the end of the world.

Then a doctor came into the room. Chloë was in her hospital bed, resting after the MRI. The doctor took me aside and quietly told me they had spotted a large mass in her brain.

My world stopped. Everything went black and I thought I might faint. Couldn't he have suggested I sit down before he gave me such terrible news? He said it could be brain cancer or it could be benign, he had nothing to go on. But he believed it was in her best interest to fly her to UCSF and have her diagnosed. And probably operated on right away to remove the mass.

My ex-husband met me and Chloë at the hospital. I had to relay the doctor's words to him and he just about lost it there in that room. He looked like he was about to jump right out of his skin, or maybe out the hospital room window. I did my best to remind him we would get the best care available for Chloë, and that we didn't know what was going on yet. We needed to stay as positive as possible and hold on to hope. But I knew full well this was easier said than done. I was screaming inside, starting to despair. I knew why her father looked the way he did.

He flew with Chloë to UCSF while my mom brought Gwen to me and we drove down to San Francisco together. We let our minds go to the worst places possible. We were a total collective emotional mess. Gwen reminds me sometimes that my mom was so stressed she was a distracted driver on our journey south. She swears her grandma ran two red lights and almost hit a pedestrian in the street along the way. But, could I blame her? We were just trying to get to Chloë as fast as we could. Luckily no one was harmed in the process.

When we got to UCSF and opened the door to Chloë's hospital room, we received the best news we could ask for. It was not cancer! They needed to prep her for brain surgery, which was absolutely terrifying, but as soon as they took the cancer aspect off the table my heart lifted to the high heavens. I was elated. Entirely and utterly thankful!

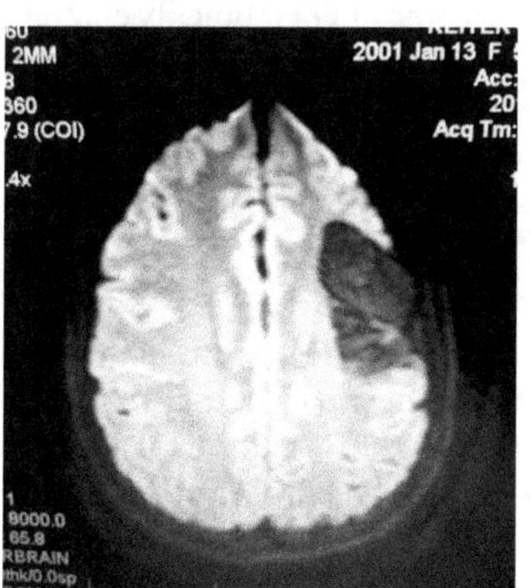

Chloë's beautiful, slightly damaged brain.

The next day things got even better; no brain surgery needed, either! A team of neurologists crowded into Chloë's hospital room to tell us the amazing news and to explain her MRI piece by piece. It turned out that Chloë had suffered some type of stroke in babyhood, or maybe even in utero. It could have been due to my difficult pregnancy with her. The placenta wore out too quickly and calcified. This meant the baby didn't get the proper amount of nutrients throughout the gestation period. My first-born came into the world at four pounds, twelve ounces. But I had no idea until twelve years later that she might have been born with brain damage or endured the damage early in infancy.

The only thing I've ever thought of that might have caused a stroke-like incident in Chloë's brain is when she stuck a key in a light socket at three years old. I tried to keep all sockets baby proofed, but this particular spot was higher up on the wall, out of reach of my six-month-old baby, Gwen. Mischievous Chloë was playing with a set of keys one day, when I heard a disturbing sound. I jumped up from my chair and looked over to where she was. She stood there holding the key oddly close to the light socket and looking dazed and wild-eyed. I was pretty damn positive I knew where the key had just been. I freaked out and took the keys from her little hand. Relieved she was alive.

She always reminds me of a fairytale princess. A strong one, with sass.

In the year that followed her stay at UCSF, Chloë had two more seizures. A bit milder than the initial one. Still scary, but not 911 scary. I knew what was happening and I now had emergency medicine for her in case she didn't come out of it quickly enough. I think I had PTSD for about four years following the onset of the episodes. Nighttime was never the same. I checked on Chloë at least three times a night like she was a newborn. Made sure she was breathing. Made sure she hadn't fallen out of bed. No more top bunk or baths. Now she had to sleep closer to the floor and only take showers with the bathroom door unlocked, just in case. Doctors' orders.

Even though I still have a terrible fear of Chloë experiencing seizures again, I live every day in gratitude for how well she is doing. The only way you would know she has major brain damage is, she can't put her own earring backs on. And she has a hard time clipping her nails. The right side of her body is a bit weaker than the left, and when she needs her finger pricked to check her iron levels, she tells the nurse to choose one of the fingers on her right hand. That way she feels it less. She has learned to turn her disadvantages in her favor. Such a strong girl. She amazes me daily.

Chapter 45

Seeing Red

I woke up in a pool of my own blood. No, I wasn't the victim of an attempted murder in the dead of night, I was having a crazy-heavy period. The kind that nothing but a full-on adult diaper could save you from. Sidenote: I refuse to wear adult diapers. I am not a baby, nor an elderly person who has lost all use of my bodily functions. But when it comes to profuse bleeding sometimes the struggle is *real.*

The worst is when you're at the office, swamped with phone calls and customers and you are worried that when you get up there's gonna be a red spot on your chair that's not spilled Kool-Aid. I don't miss the days in high school when you're extra self conscious about everything as it is and you have to wait till the bell rings to run to the restroom to see if your teenage life has been ruined along with your favorite jeans.

A few months ago I was again having an overly heavy cycle and I fell asleep on the living room couch. Around 2:00 a.m. I awoke and tried to get up to pee, made it halfway to the bathroom and collapsed in the hallway right outside the door. I was in extreme pain and when I was finally able to get up on my hands and knees and on to my feet again, I stared at myself in the mirror and a ghost looked back. All the blood had drained from my face. I guess because all the red stuff from my entire body was indisposed in another location at the moment. Running away as fast as it could from some unforeseen danger.

I was able to relieve my bladder. Then as I tried to walk back to the couch, I collapsed on the floor *again.* Too weak and hurting too badly to stay upright. And to be honest, at this point I got really scared. Scared that maybe something terrible was wrong with me. Maybe I was dying. Right there on the carpet. Worried my husband and kids would find me in the light of dawn and have to make funeral arrangements.

Thankfully, surprise, surprise! I did not die that night. But I did ask a doctor who taught at the community college if my symptoms were normal. I apologized for asking him about such an "over sharing" topic. But I needed a little peace of mind that I wouldn't bleed to death the next time I tried to lie down and go to sleep. The doctor smiled his usual, kind and understanding smile, and said, "Yeah, sometimes that happens. The blood can pull too quickly from other areas of the body and leave you feeling pretty weak." Well, I'll say. Ain't that the truth.

Periods from hell are not fun. But what about periods from heaven? Have you ever heard of a woman experiencing something like that? I want one of those. Complete with a build up of PMS from Nirvana. Yes, please. I could get behind these welcome upgrades for women who already have enough of a bleeding heart. We don't need to bleed so much from other places, too.

The menstrual cycle is an odd phenomenon. There's still so much stigma associated with it. I'm convinced that if men dealt with it monthly instead of women, by now they would have created a law that people on their periods must stay home one week a month to rest and recuperate. If men had the periods, menstruation would be "cool." Something to brag about and compare to other men's cycles and such. But since it's a woman's burden, well, it's considered embarrassing, something to hide, something to be whispered about under cover of night.

Generation after generation of women and girls have exchanged pads and tampons in classrooms and parking lots like they're illicit drugs or unregistered semi-automatic weapons. When they unexpectedly start their cycle and are caught empty-handed, they use their quietest voices to request a donated product from the nearest female. And in developing nations a lot of the female population doesn't even have access to feminine hygiene products. Which is a travesty. Even today in America, we fight to get feminine hygiene listed with the necessities, not the luxuries, so we can buy them and not be taxed unnecessarily. What a concept, right?

Chapter 46

Time Is Precious, and Not All Education Comes from a Textbook

I am six credits away from graduating from college. I'm going to walk in graduation next spring and receive my ten-year degree. Er, I mean my two-year degree. Wait. Why did my two-year degree take me ten years??! What happened? What's wrong with me? Ahhhhhhhhhh!

To start with, when I graduated from high school, I was so burned-out I was positive my head would explode if I ever took another academic class. I was exhausted with my life never being my own, an existence ruled by homework and stress. No thanks. On top of that, I had convinced myself I was stupid, thanks to my downturn in math during my sophomore year. What a shame I could be so easily defined by a class not in an area of my strengths.

I took eight years off between high school and college. I say off, but I was not off-duty from hard work, having had my kids so young.

Update: I just GRADUATED from college with my Associates Degree in Humanities! I donned my green cap and gown, wore bright red lipstick and proudly walked in the ceremony to accept my diploma. It's a personal goal, really, completing this milestone. I wanted to set a good example for my children. Mostly, I just wanted to cross off education from my endless to-do list. Most of my education has come from living my life, raising my kids, learning from relationship malfunctions, and following my creative path. Learning is lifelong, and I am a firm believer that degrees are not what make us intelligent. They simply signal to others that we were willing, briefly in my case, to jump through a few hoops and put in a lot of hours doing homework on the couch. And to those who put in waaaay more hours than I did, and came away with a much higher degree, congratulations! That is truly awesome and you have my respect and admiration. Higher degrees, however, are not my path. I am not ashamed. I am not sorry. And I am not going to lie and say that someday I will go back to school. BOOM! Arianna out.

Chapter 47

Back Off, Old Man

He used to frequent the gym in Weaverville where I worked. He was old. Like really old. And I was twenty-four. His name was Ron, and he loved to tell people about his acting career in Hollywood during his younger years. He spoke as if he was always on stage. An exagerated Shakespearean quality in his voice and word inflections. Even when he said the most commonplace phrases.

He took a liking to me when we first met, and I noticed he was a flirt with all the women he ran into. I think he fancied himself quite the Casanova. Once he attended a showing of a musical I was in with his button-up shirt noticeably unbuttoned too far. Gray chest hair showing as if he wore it like a gold chain or a flashy tattoo.

Ron always greeted me with such grandeur. He was really quite sweet. But I noticed he pushed the envelope with his flirting and I became more watchful to not encourage his attentions toward me. He once told me I had such beautiful lips. Something weird, comparing them to rosebuds or rose petals. The memory is fuzzy, but still creepy when I think of it.

One time he had a script reading at his house and invited me and several other people in the arts community from our little town. It was odd, rather uncomfortable. But he kept his behavior appropriate, and I got myself through the evening wondering why I put myself through it in the first place.

Shortly after, Ron and I were cast in a dramatic production together. It was an adaptation of a British play written by the husband of my college art teacher. This was the production where I realized I wasn't cut out for acting. But I didn't realize it in time to back out. I went forward head-on. Even learning a British accent and wearing uncomfortable Victorian style dresses. I loved my cast. Working with so many wonderful people was great. Even the beloved local veterinarian had a role. One of the nicest guys you could ever meet.

During an onstage run through one day, I had to rehearse a scene with Ron. We sat on a small antique loveseat exchanging our lines in front of our director and fellow castmates. After I delivered one of my lines, Ron began reciting his next one, but made an impromptu change. He reached his hand out in front of my face and then touched, yes *touched,* my lips. And before I could even register my horror and recoil, he let his hand fall down in such a way to conveniently slide firmly across my left breast.

What. The. Fuck. I was dumbstruck. All I could do was finish out the scene and get out of that damn theatre as quickly as possible. I called my director the next day and complained. I was angry. He offered to talk to Ron. I didn't take him up on it. But I told him that if anything like it happened again I sure as heck would. I just needed to vent and ask him to watch Ron's actions more closely while we were on stage together. I was so grossed-out.

The rest of the rehearsals were awkward, and I did not speak to Ron in any way unless we delivered our lines opposite each other. He tried to talk to me after a run through, saying, "I notice there's been a change in you. Are you okay? Was it something I did?" I didn't even want to give him the satisfaction of a response, but I couldn't help myself. I replied, "You know damn well what you did Ron. Don't touch me. Don't talk to me. Just don't. Ever again." And boy did I fucking mean those words. I tried to put as much poison in them as I could. And I hoped he felt the sting.

It's funny, isn't it? How something that seems to be so inconsequential to an old man can make a young woman have to deal with a disturbing memory seared into her brain for the rest of her life. I still see Ron once in a while when I pass through my beloved hometown, and I do everything in my power to go nowhere near him. And especially to avoid eye contact. He's just one more man from my past who made me feel a little less like a person and a little more like an object to touch as he pleased. I'm really not into that shit.

If I'm lucky, someday I'll hear he was in yet another small town production, and an old woman he had no attraction to conveniently got too close during practice and grabbed his crotch. It would be very fitting karma, and I would relish the thought of him feeling objectified the way he objectified me. As I write this I realize just how vindictive I really am. But only in extreme cases. I've probably already mentioned this, but forgiveness just isn't my bag, baby. I don't wish Ron any sinister harm, only a strong taste of his own medicine. That would do the trick.

Chapter 48

Felicia Berland Hyatt

My grandfather's first cousin, Felicia Berland Hyatt, survived the Holocaust and told her story in a memoir called "Close Calls." The reason my grandpa's cousin had the last name of "Berland" and my grandfather's last name was "Berlandt" with a "t" was because my unique Grandpa Herman added the "t" to his name himself. He said he thought it made it seem more "authentic." Whatever that means.

When I read Felicia's memoir, I was left dumbfounded. She was shockingly brave. She came close to certain death many times and yet came out on the other side. Vibrant and alive.

During part of her journey, Felicia was a nanny to the two small children of a Nazi officer. She had to pose as a non-Jew, knowing that any second she might be found out and executed on the spot. Her mother never made it through. They lost each other at a certain point when her mom became too weak to travel on. They never saw each other again. That part kills me.

Felicia's father—my great-great uncle—left Poland for New York City just before all the Jews in their area were rounded up by the Germans. Father and daughter were reunited after the war was over.

If reincarnation exists, I've often wondered if I was a small child who was murdered in the Holocaust. Either that, or the genetics that run through my veins carry Holocaust "recollections" that haunt me. It may sound strange, but I feel like I have memories of being small and having everything of importance ripped away from me.

I have weird issues with photographs, feeling like they are all going to be ruined or lost somehow, so I try not to get too attached. This could be attributed to my depression issues, but I can't shake the feeling that it goes deeper than that. It's a gruesome thought, but I feel like I died in a gas chamber around eighty years ago. It's just too strong of an intuition to push out of my mind.

A big regret is never making it to New York City to meet Felicia before she passed away. She lived into her nineties. I would have loved to give her a hug and thank her for sharing her story. Knowing she was part of my family gives me unique strength to draw on when I need to conjure up extra courage. If she could survive hell on earth, I should be able to survive damn near anything.

Chapter 49

Dang, Did I Really Just Say That?

It was the summer after I left my ex-husband. I needed a job and one of my best girlfriends from childhood was running an environmental summer camp in my hometown. To be honest, I wasn't on fire about taking the position, but I needed to start being a big girl and providing for myself and my daughters, so…

One of my duties was to pick up and coordinate all the day's meals for the little rascals. Who would have thought something that simple could stress me out so bad? But, I've probably already mentioned this: I'm not normal. The things that should be easy are hard for me. The things that should be hard are easy. Not to overgeneralize: climbing Mt. Everest should be hard, and for me it would be impossible, because someone could offer me a billion dollars to attempt it and my answer would be: "No thanks, I'm good."

Now, let me tell you about the most terrifying and embarrassing moment I remember about this job. The camp arranged to take all the kids river rafting. Seems harmless, right? Wrong. It was freakin' scary. The rapids were way too big for my comfort zone. And even with rafting guides I didn't feel comfortable with the risk we were taking with other peoples' children. Kids who were depending on us to keep them safe. I should note, however, that my boss followed protocol perfectly, and this is in no way a criticism of her. She's amazing and incredibly competent at anything and everything she sets her mind to. I want to make that abundantly clear. I'm just a big scaredy cat when it comes to even slightly risky behavior around water. It's my issue. I have a lot of them.

One of my many phobias is the thought of falling overboard and getting stuck *underneath* the raft. Not being able to find my way to the surface of the water. Until my lifeless body eventually just pops up several miles downstream. With an expression written on my dead face that screams, "I fucking *knew* this was not going to end well!" They tell you if you were to find yourself in that predicament (of being stuck under the raft) to just, "Keep crawling along underneath the raft until you get out from under it." River guides state this advice in the same way they might say, "If your shoe becomes untied as you walk down the trail, just bend down and re-tie it." I mean, wow, thanks Captain Obviously-gonna-get-me-drowned. Good Lord.

Despite my trepidation, I tried to be a good sport and a good employee. I loved the camp's spirit of adventure, but my intuition was telling me that my participation in this particular activity was a baaaaad idea. We floated along, minding our own business and I put on a brave face for my little crew. Our river guide was probably twenty years old, but he looked no more than twelve. That was comforting. Twelve years old and he was a cocky son of a bitch. He got us caught amongst blackberry vines along the edge of the river once or twice. Then we apparently veered down the wrong side of a "Y" that the river made around a small island. The rapids suddenly became more violent and our raft got stuck on a shallow spot right on the edge of a crazy drop into a big pool. Our obviously seasoned (this is sarcasm, in case you can't tell) river guide nonchalantly announced that we would all need to jump out of the raft and swim, because the raft was about to tip over and evacuate us whether we liked it or not. At this point I'd had it. I was stressed out beyond belief, I was scared for our lives, and this freakin' river guide was telling us to get ready for our raft to completely forsake us when we needed it the most.

This is when it happened. A moment that lives in infamy in my mind and probably in several small children's minds, too. The moment when my fight-or-flight survival mode kicked in and my rational brain checked out. The raft was tipping more and more, and again the guide told us to JUMP! To my horror, I heard myself yell at the top of my lungs, "*JESUS FUCKING CHRIST!!!*" It was like in the movies where all of a sudden the character yelling is in slow motion and their voice is slowed down so much they sound like an old man. But yes, it was I who uttered this phrase. Right after I emanated these unholy words, our raft miraculously dislodged from whatever was hanging it up and we were smooth sailing again. In that almost peaceful moment, I would have liked to pretend I did not say the three words I said. I would have also liked to fake a grand mal seizure to get out of such an uncomfortable situation. But as I looked at all the little faces staring up at me, their big eyes said it all. They heard every word I yelled and were now wondering if I was some sort of spawn of Satan.

At this point the only thing to do was exactly what I did. I looked right at these small, frightened human beings and said, "I'm sorry kids, *that* was inappropriate."

Chapter 50

Paris, Mon Amour

I turned sixteen at the top of the Eiffel Tower, eating flan. I cherish so many memories from this trip. It was organized by a teacher at my high school who somehow pulled off a three-week excursion to Paris in the springtime. I look back and don't even know how much it cost my parents out of pocket. I am thankful they allowed me to go. Considering the fact that my sister at sixteen moved to India for a year, maybe my three week adventure seemed mild to them. Maybe they were relieved it was all I wanted.

The second we touched down in France my entire life perspective changed. I was bombarded by beauty. I was also bombarded by sweet cream butter and baguettes. The best I'd ever had. We subsisted on them while we lived like starving artists on the nineteenth story of a Paris apartment building. At night we looked through the kitchen and living room windows to see the Eiffel Tower shining like a heavenly beacon. I was not raised to subscribe to any specific religion, but I can easily say that this trip will go down in my life as one of my most spiritual experiences, second only to my recent wedding. It was as if I could feel the centuries of artists, architects and sculptors gone by. The beautiful spirit of creativity oozed out of the cracks in the cobblestone streets. I was overcome by the

---

Notre Dame did not disappoint.

living history around every corner of the city. And the disappointing part was realizing how generic so much of America is. Young and naive. There are aspects of beauty in America, but they are hard to find. In Europe they are in every detail of daily life. As I say this, I am aware that hidden behind all that incredible beauty is a huge amount of death, destruction and suffering. Those massive buildings didn't build themselves, and I don't think every contributor was a willing participant. Same goes for the Taj Mahal and the pyramids of Egypt. Why is it that so many of the most breathtaking wonders of the world are also symbols of destruction to individual lives? It's hard to reconcile this sad truth.

Paris was a type of coming of age for me; it was also the first time I ever drank alcohol. And, obviously, we were legally able to buy it there. My friends and I would stock up on wine and go sit beneath the tower. We would drink and stare in awe all around us. Magical doesn't even come close to describing how it felt. It was as if the whole world had suddenly come into focus in my eyes. There was so much more to life and human potential than I had ever realized. The effects of the alcohol allowed me to feel more connected to my friends. It was like I saw them for the first time, and for the first time I felt like they saw me. This was major for a teen like myself, who had always dealt with debilitating insecurity, stresses about weight and worth. Always trying to figure out where I belonged and who I was.

In telling of my travels, I'm not advocating teen drinking but simply sharing the effect of this adventure on me. I am thankful I don't seem to be wired to be an alcoholic or an addict, if I had been, my story could have turned out much darker.

Speaking of dark addiction stories, during an outing we visited the burial place of Jim Morrison. He has an odd final resting place in a Paris cemetery. It was a strange field trip, but intriguing in its own way. I hope he is resting peacefully and eating Parisian pastries while getting his portrait painted by a French artist up in Rock and Roll Heaven.

There is a song that rings eternal in my ears. "One Headlight" by the Wallflowers. It haunts me when I hear it, and transports me back to the Palace of Versailles, and its Hall of Mirrors. The apartment overlooking the city. The feelings too big to understand. It takes me back to laughing with my friend Nicole, enamored with the song as much as I was. I love Jacob Dylan's voice. Somewhere between ethereal serenity and heavy overcast. That's where his mysterious sound can be found. He sang the soundtrack to this life-changing event. He took an already incredible experience to the next level, the way only a story-telling singer-songwriter can do.

Chapter 51

Superglued Heart

Every now and then I am struck with this deep fear surrounding infidelity. I'm overly familiar with the subject from both sides of the coin. When I was married the first time, my husband cheated on me at least once that I know of. I'm afraid there may have been many times I did not know of. I don't want, or need, to know now.

Then in my next long-term relationship, I was the unfaithful one. Remember? I told you I'd explain. And yes, I'm speaking again about my ex-boyfriend, David. This came as a shock to me. I loved the guy so much and became needy for more attention from him. He was coming out of a marriage as well, but he seemed less over his. Probably because his wife had left him instead of the other way around. For some reason I fell so hard for this man. Stupidly hard. He only wanted to see me about fifty percent of the time. We would spend three or four nights together during the week and never see each other on the weekends because that was when his daughters were with him, and apparently he viewed me as some sort of horrible person who might corrupt his children. Actually no, I'm kidding, but that's how it made me feel. One of the real reasons is because his ex-wife was *actually a horrible person*, and would have a conniption fit if she found out I had visited with her children. So, needless to say we started off this relationship on the basis of his ex-wife being in charge of it, rather than him or me. Or ideally, both of us.

As time went on I felt lonely during many of the nights I spent without him. Especially the nights when my girls were with their father. It was such a weird feeling, having met a man that, by all accounts, was incredibly kind, hard working, somewhat intelligent (I say only somewhat because in the end he left me. What smart man does that?) yet was not willing to give me all of him, just part. I built up resentment quickly. I even built up resentment towards his new puppy, because as soon as he got her, he would go home from my place to his place even earlier in the evenings. Even his puppy was better prioritized in his life than I was. I love dogs, but give me a break.

This was during a time when I was experiencing some serious complications from stress, mostly from my job as a special needs aid at that elementary school I told you about. My jaw was seizing up due to anger and frustration I wasn't able to wash away when I came home from work. I had constant, intense neck pain.

I saw a chiropractor for a few adjustments. Someone recommended it and I figured it was worth a shot. Part of me wishes I could go back in time and unmake that decision, but that's not going to happen, and that's how this whole mess started. The chiropractor took some X-rays, pinpointed what was going on with my neck and did his best to figure out how to fix my jaw issue. I look back and realize in horror that he planned to date me from the moment I walked into his office. I didn't see it at first. I could tell that he was kind of a schmoozer and probably fancied himself a ladies' man, but that was it. It didn't seem like any big deal.

After a few more appointments, he began asking seemingly harmless questions about my life, and especially about my relationship. I was devoted to my boyfriend and felt strongly that he was the one for me. I told him I was deeply in love with David. I wasn't trying to hide that fact in the least. The chiropractor asked questions about what I found difficult in my relationship. Really, the only things I said were related to lack of time spent with my boyfriend. I was honest about that part being hard for me and I couldn't understand why David didn't want to spend as much time with me as I did with him.

I've never gotten around to researching the psychology of it, but I think this chiropractor was purposely exacerbating the weakest link in my relationship so that my wound would get bigger, bleed a little more and a little more during each appointment, until he could be the one to apply the first aid.

The chiropractor invited me to his house to try a new sound wave therapy he said he didn't have a license for in the office. I knew he was coming on to me, but for some stupid reason I thought I could handle it. After all, he was not the man I wanted. The only man I truly wanted was the man I was already with…half the time.

As you may have already guessed, I went to Mr. Chiropractor's house and yes, I slept with him. Against all my better judgment. It didn't happen the second I got there. I was there for a few hours beforehand. He tried the sound wave machine on my neck, and then started kissing me in the same spot. I didn't want him. But I guess I was just attracted to him enough to not stop him. I had hit a rebellious brick wall of understanding that my boyfriend wanted me to be devoted to him but didn't want to commit to us actually living our lives together. We were together only a few days at a time and then I had to live like a single person again. I admit this was an immature viewpoint on my part. And I feel David's fear of commitment was immature, too.

I have gone around and around in my head to make sure I don't simply blame my own infidelity on my partner at the time. Logically, I do know I had a choice and I made the wrong one. One that caused a lot of pain. Both to my boyfriend when I broke the news to him a week later, and to the girlfriend of Mr. Chiropractor. It's a terrible feeling when you have a conscience and a strong moral compass of right and wrong and you find yourself going completely against both in one fell swoop. You can never take it back. All you can do is deal with the aftermath and come clean. A lot of people say it's best to not tell your partner if you've been unfaithful. They swear it will only do more harm than good, and if you know you still want to stay with that partner you might as well do just that and keep your mouth shut. When I've heard this argument I've always wondered, "How the fuck does anyone with a conscience do this?" A relationship is supposed to be based on truth and love, and a similar sense of humor. Relationships are not meant to be built upon lies and deceit.

So, I did the dreadfully wrong thing then had to deal with the dreadful fallout that erupted from it. I'm certain my infidelity played a role in my boyfriend's breakup with me a few years later. It was the same pattern as with my ex-husband. I found out he had been unfaithful, it broke my heart. I stayed with him but grew more and more distant and less and less devoted. We had mountains of problems already, but the nail in the coffin was the proof of infidelity. Same as with the boyfriend I cheated on. My infidelity was the nail in the coffin of an already messed-up relationship. I'm glad now that David left me. It allowed me to become happier than I could have ever imagined. It allowed me to find Lefty. It allowed Lefty to find me. And I must say, we are both pretty great finds.

This brings me to my main concern. Now that I am remarried, I recognize I have old wounds that won't heal. Because infidelity played a central role in my other two long-term relationships, how am I supposed to feel like it's never going to come up in this marriage? I love my husband more deeply than I have ever loved any man before, and I am committed to doing anything and everything I need to do to stay one hundred percent faithful. I've learned these tough lessons the hard way and don't need to relearn them in my new marriage. But I have a lingering fear of being cheated on. All I have to do is think about that coming up in my marriage now and my eyes get wet and I feel this catch in my chest that hurts.

When we love someone and devote ourselves to them we give them so much power. This power is beautiful and awe-inspiring. This power can be used for so much good. But trust is hard. And it's scary as hell. And I think one of my deepest fears is allowing myself to be played a fool. I worry about someone cheating and me *never finding out.* It happens all the time. *Why does this kind of thing happen all the time?* Why doesn't everyone feel the same need to tell their partner if they fuck up (literally)? This I will never know.

And I want to make something clear: I love Lefty more unconditionally than I've ever loved a man before. I'm not insinuating that he has ever cheated on me or will ever cheat. My fears are not specific to him and my fears are not his fault. My fears simply *are.* They exist, and will probably never go away. I'm fully aware that I have a superglued heart. And I vow here and now to get more intensive counseling on this topic. It's worth a shot. For all I know he may have the same fears regarding me. When we first started dating I was open with him about being unfaithful to my previous partner.

He tends to be a lot more private about previous relationships. That's okay. But fear sucks. And I hope in our marriage, love wins. And will always win.

Please God, let this be the case and give me faith that Lefty and I don't have to learn these lessons together. I don't want to walk through the fire with him, I simply want to bask in the warmth of our strong connection and appreciation for each other. I want to love him with an open heart. A heart that can pretend it has never been hurt before. And if ever we *do* find ourselves in the midst of an inferno due to infidelity or any other major issue, please let us have an endless water supply to put it out. To heal *together.* Please let this be our never ending love. Lefty + Arianna forever. I can't handle another breakup. And god damnit, I *LOVE HIM SOOOOO!!!*

Chapter 52

Oh, I'm Sorry, You Expected Me to Be Perfect?

I suppose this is a good time to lay out something as a result of my infidelity with Mr. Chiropractor. When I owned up to what I had done, one of the yuckiest times in my life, one of my best girlfriends shocked the heck out of me by behaving in a way I couldn't have foreseen. Her name is, well, I will call her Dana, and she and I were incredibly close friends for about seven years. She is a stunningly beautiful woman. Tall and curvy, with long black curly hair and huge eyes that shine with fierce fire. Speaking of fierceness, she is either fiercely protective of you when you are in her life, or fiercely vindictive and accusatory towards you. There's nothing in between. And I've been on the receiving end of both her approaches.

As most girlfriends do, over the years we often discussed the men in our lives. Good times and bad. It helps to talk about relationship problems with supportive people who will simply listen without trying to run your life. Dana always tried to run everyone's life a bit, but it never bothered me. I just took it to mean that she cared about me and wanted to see me live a healthy, happy existence. So, I discussed how unhappy I was that David didn't want to devote enough time to our relationship. I remember her being concerned with how unhappy I sounded as time wore on. But I could never, ever have anticipated what she actually did when she found out about my big mistake.

When I broke the awful news to David, he was incredibly upset, as anyone would be when cheated on. We broke up for a time while trying to sort out the mess. He worked as a special needs teacher at an elementary school. A different school than the one where I worked. Dana and he were old friends from high school, and it just so happened that her daughter attended David's school. Apparently Dana ran into David one morning and asked him what was wrong. He told her. And Dana proceeded to tell him that I planned all along to hurt him in the way I did. She said she wasn't surprised by my infidelity because basically I was a terrible person in her eyes, and I had no conscience. WTF? Really, Dana? You knew me how long? And now I find out that you never really knew me at all.

I was so flustered. I couldn't figure out how she could throw me under the bus like that, then make sure, once it ran over me, to knife me in the back for good measure. She was out for blood and I couldn't understand why. She couldn't bother to say to David, "Wow, I'm so sorry she did that to you! I need to catch up with that girl and see what's going on with her." No, she had to immediately think I was simply a malicious human being with malicious tendencies and no remorse. This could not have been further from the truth. I felt powerless in an already nightmarish situation. Sure, most of it was my own doing, but who expects a best friend to pour salt on the wound of the worst relationship disaster she's ever walked through? The only thing I could think of is that maybe she was secretly in love with David, too. Maybe she saw this as her chance to swoop in and take him for her own. Who knows? That's my soap opera theory, anyway.

Even though I was shocked by Dana's behavior, I tried to reach out and talk to her, hoping we could clear the air if we each tried to better understand the other. She wasn't interested. She acted like I had cheated on *her*. A drama queen to the max, I saw what I had always worried about in the back of my mind during our friendship. She often spoke badly of people whom I knew to be nice, decent human beings. This is always a bad sign, because you know that someday it is going to be your turn. Well, I guess this was my turn to be the bad guy in her eyes. Everything was black or white to her, no room for gray. So I had to accept that she was never going to forgive me or try to understand me, and she was never going to love me again. It hurt like hell. I hate losing friends. Good ones, truly good ones, are hard to find, and even harder to maintain throughout life. People get busy, grow apart, realize the other was an idiot all along, you name it. But I just didn't see this one coming. It was sad, because I would have done so much to stay close to her. I loved her dearly. I still feel angry when I think about Dana, but mostly I wish her well and miss her laugh and her warm hugs. She has a cozy little place in my heart, even though that place may or may not have a few signs on the wall that say, "What the fuck, girl? Grow up and love me again. I'm waiting, and ready to love you back."

Chapter 53

Black Dress

The last thing I'll say about my heartwrenching cheating incident is this: One night shortly after David and I patched things up and were trying to make our relationship work, I had the most vivid dream. I dreamed we were getting married, but everything felt off. I was running crazy late getting myself together for the ceremony. I felt sick to my stomach and when I went looking in a closet to find a gown to put on, all I could find was a black wedding dress. Even in my dream I knew exactly what that meant. I knew David and I were never going to survive what I had done to us.

I remember waking up feeling tragically sad. There was no way to misconstrue the information relayed to me. Kind of like that dream I had about the mountain lion on the river bank, before my first marriage. Both these dreams foretold the future, right at times when I desperately did not want to accept the facts. But, I look back knowing what I know now, and I would not change a thing.

The best days in our lives would never happen if not for the devastating circumstances that tear everything down and force us to re-build. Everything I experienced led me to meeting Lefty. And the dress I wore when I married him was white. Classic. Symbolic of hope, life, the dove of peace. Love and light. That is what my life is encompassed by now. I appreciate the good so much more, having known the bad so intimately.

Chapter 54

Teenagers

I have three of them. My step-son, Cameron. My younger daughter, Gwen, and my oldest daughter, Chloë. Where did the time go? Who the fuck put me in a time machine and pushed fast forward??! And why did no one prepare me for how hard it is to let go of worrying about my kids every single second of every day, even though they are getting bigger?

I feel like I graduated from high school five years ago. It's been almost twenty! I'm not impressed with this thing called aging. I refuse. Let's freeze this moment, minus thirty pounds, plus ten million bucks. Okay? Okay. I mean seriously. I'm tired.

Everytime I think I've seen the worst of raising teens, something comes up that tops the previous horror I hoped was rock bottom. I hate to sound jaded, but I honestly feel shocked every other day at the issues that arise. Feelings of being wholly overwhelmed by my lack of preparedness during this timeframe as a mother makes me sick to my stomach. And I often sink into this dark abyss that swallows me up, shame and all. Yet, when the darkness realizes that it cannot digest me, it inevitably spits me back out, and right there beside me lands all that same shame, guilt and sense of complete incompetence. Talk about a fucking drag. That vicious cyle of thought that says to us:

You can't do this.

You don't know how.

Your efforts will only make matters worse, so why are you even trying?

Oppressive mental states that consume our parental identity are corrosive and counterintuitive to being a functional mother to our teenagers, who, despite how much they try to say otherwise, still need us. Almost more than they needed us when they were little kids running around in princess dresses. Chasing butterflies that land on wild daisies growing as tall as the hair on the top of their heads.

If given the opportunity, I would not go back in time and relive the younger years of my childrens' childhoods. I wouldn't. But do I miss the simplicity of the problems in their lives back then? Yes. Do I miss that simpler time when I could pick them up and put them on my hip when they cried? Wipe their tears away with a flick of my finger and a soft voice in their ear? Double yes. But the actuality of time is ever forward moving. Time doesn't stop for us. Even when we need it to. And so we must learn to cheat time itself, even if just a bit, by staying up extra late talking to our daughters about boy problems and cyber bullying. About how to spot the red flags that indicate someone is not safe to date. About how to conduct themselves in the face of incredible pain due to other kids deciding it's ok to be entertained by their most humiliating moments.

When people say, "It's a crazy world out there," it's one of the biggest understatements one can make. Oh how I wish it was just crazy. Like a crazy uncle who always makes us laugh, or a day filled with chaotic but superficial hindrances. Just crazy might be ok. But it's the downright dangers and bad intentions from others my children will have to watch out for that make me ill. There is so much good and so much depravity in this "crazy" world of ours. And my prayer every night for my children is that the scales of their lives will always tip towards the *good.*

Chapter 55

He Had No Right

"Ask a man what his greatest fear is about serving jail time, and he will almost inevitably say he fears being raped. What can we deduce from the fact that jail is to men what life is to so many women?"
– Soraya Chemaly

The alcohol hit me unusually hard that night. And why on earth I let him bring me that first drink, I'll never know. I guess I was naive and waaaaaay overly trusting at the time. Recently divorced, rather lonely, a bit lost. I had this false sense of security because he was an acquaintance of my brother's. They had played music together in various bands for years. Fucked-up musicians come a dime a dozen (It's okay, I can say that. I'm a singer. Ha!) but seriously, this guy was *really* fucked up. I never fully blacked out that night, but I remember feeling like I was in a waking dream. He took me back to his place after we left the bar. We went to his bedroom and he put me on the bed and tried to have sex with me immediately. No build up, no tenderness or romance, no nothing except trying to be inside of me without a condom. I stopped him. I remember saying no and that he needed to use protection. I took one out of my purse and handed it to him. He disregarded me and kept trying to enter me anyway. I think I was in and out of consciousness. And I only had two drinks at the bar. I can hold my liquor. There was something else accentuating the effects.

Long story short, this guy got tired of me telling him he could not have sex with me without a condom, so he flipped me over on the bed, onto my belly, and proceeded to put his cock in my ass. Without my consent, without a condom. I was so out of it at the time that I couldn't find the words to object, but it quickly became more and more painful. Too painful. I vividly remember saying, "Okay, that's enough. We have to stop. You have to stop!" But he did not stop. Just kept going at me like I was some disposable blowup doll. Like I was not human, like I didn't matter, like I was a piece of trash at his disposal for his "needs." And then...all of a sudden he *did* stop. Not because he came to his senses, but because he came inside of me and had no more use for my body. Because that's all I was to him, a body. I was still in and out of consciousness. I didn't have full use of my thoughts or extremities. It was as if there was an electrical current pulsing through me, but someone kept turning the breaker on and off, over and over. I felt like a zombie. I almost wish I had been. At least I could have left him bleeding and brainless on the floor.

He put me back in his car and drove me to my best friend's house where I was staying for the weekend. Dropped me off and drove away. Fuzzy red tail lights faded into the distance while my electricity continued to short circuit and surge in an odd, eerie rhythm. I don't remember going inside Kaela's house that night. Don't remember laying my head on the pillow in her guest room, or falling asleep. But I do remember telling her about the incident the next morning.

She asked me, "So, do you feel like he took advantage of you?"

I responded with a confused, "Yeah, it was really weird."

I was in denial about the full extent of what he had done to me. I still felt out of it. Having no clarity of mind yet, I actually wanted to see him again. Crazy stupid, right? I didn't want to believe that he had intentionally drugged and raped me. When it washed over me, that thought made me shake with anger and horror, and I pushed it out of my mind, hoping I was confused and wrong. During that next day, even in the midst of extreme pain from what he did to me, I tried to see this douchebag again. Attempting to run from all this fear that was swirling up inside of me. He made lame excuses as to why he couldn't see me. It wasn't until a day or two later, when my brain and emotional fog cleared up, that I solidly realized *this motherfucker raped me*. Plain and fucking simple.

When I came to my senses, though briefly, I emailed a former girlfriend of my brother's and told her what had happened. She had known this jerk for years. She was shocked and didn't really believe that he did what I said he did to me. She said, "That really doesn't sound like him, Arianna. I've known him a long time and I don't think he would do something like that to you or anyone else." It wasn't the comforting response I was seeking. I sent this creep a scathing email telling him exactly what he did to me and how wrong it was. I let loose on him. I didn't hold back. He, of course, wrote a response with crocodile tears in his words, saying he was so sorry, but that I was completely mistaken. He never tried to hurt me. Didn't hear me saying stop...blaah, blaah, blaah, fucking blaah, blaah, blaah.

Here's where you might get upset with me in this twisted fiasco: I walked back my accusatory attitude with this guy over a period of time after the incident. I'm pretty sure I would have had a full-blown mental and emotional breakdown if I had continued to validate my feelings about what had taken place. I didn't want to admit to myself that I had been a victim of rape. The technical term for what was done to me would probably be date rape, but don't you agree that saying the words "date" and "rape" together kind of "sanitizes" the rape? Date rape sounds so benign. I refuse to call it that.

The reason you may be disappointed in me, perhaps even disgusted with my lack of judgement, is that I eventually agreed to see this guy again, after he reached out to me several times. Unfortunately it was not under the condition of "me zombie, he zombie lunch." I believe I was searching for a way to take back my power in this unsanitary mess. I believe my need to see him again came from not wanting to see myself as a victim. In order to achieve this, I had to downplay what he did to me, and kinda-sorta-maybe-fake-believe that he didn't mean it. He maybe didn't mean to drug me and rape me in the ass while I was yelling in pain for him to stop. Maybe it was an accidental rape. Is that a thing? Regardless, I had a need to "date" him off and on for a while longer. He never raped me again, but I shamefully admit I slept with him a handful of times over the following two or three months. He was a super-weird dude who did too much cocaine and taught music to children at his private music school. He had a creepy nervous tic. Was it the cocaine? Was it his dark soul trying to squeeze out the evil, one tic at a time? God knows, but it made an impression. Not the good kind.

Eventually, around the time this excuse for a man sent me a late-night text telling me he loved me, I was done with him. I took glee in knowing that, in his own fucked up way, maybe he actually had grown to love me, and I had the power to sever ties. Right in that exact second. Walk away. Hurt him back, I hope. It wasn't zombie-attack/brains-painting-the-bedroom-floor-dramatic, but it was something. In an unexplainable way, I had mostly healed myself from the harm this man did to me. I don't advocate that victims of sexual violence do what I did. It may not be admirable, or even understandable. But it worked for me.

* * *

Fast forward a couple years. The top story on a local news station involved a California music teacher and a teenage girl he hired to clean his house. A picture flashed across the screen. It was him. He exposed himself to her while she was working in his kitchen. She was seventeen years old. I felt sick to my stomach. The news story went on to say that this idiot had already been in jail for assaulting a former girlfriend with a *weapon.*

I put the pieces together. This guy was a real sexual predator. No, I didn't imagine that he drugged me. No, I did not imagine that he raped me. No, I *wasn't crazy.* He was a really bad guy and I worked up the courage to call the Police Department to add myself to the list of this man's accusers. The woman who answered my call transferred me to a special investigator. I left him a voicemail. *He never called me back.*

Chapter 56

The White Girl in the Room

I was born white, grew up white, and have remained white for the entirety of my adulthood. Do I really have a choice? Of course not. But I never knew just *how white* I was until I met my husband. Being lucky enough to experience his incredible Lao culture has been one of the most amazing blessings. We eat sitting on the living room floor around a circular bamboo tray that, when not in use, hangs above our kitchen table. Sticky rice is a staple food at every meal and doubles as a utensil in most cases. You ball up a small amount of rice in your freshly washed hands, pack it tight, then dip it in papaya salad, spicy soy sauce, flavorful broiled fish, you name it. It's all so good.

Lao cooking is a beautiful art form, and my husband is quite the chef. He jokes that all he really does is "burn meat" but he's being humble. I'm sure a lot of his culinary gifts were handed down to him by his parents and other family members, but I'm also sure Lefty has perfected many of his special dishes to his unique taste.

One of his tricks is plenty of MSG in everything. He always reminds me, with a laugh, that it stands for "Makes Shit Good" and he's right. I grew up thinking MSG was some sort of evil powder that gave people headaches and caused imminent death. It has gotten a bad rap over the years. But I don't know, we are all alive and well, and the only side effect I can pinpoint is that Lefty's cooking is obscenely delicious.

Fun fact: MSG is also my stepfather's initials, which never fails to amuse me. It doesn't take much to make me laugh. He's a great guy and I love him dearly. He likes to write his initials on coolers and other such items around his house. When I see it I have to stifle my immature giggles.

Getting back to what I said about realizing just how very white I am... well, it took a different cultural perspective from the point of view of my husband and his family for me to have a window into white culture, or lack thereof. When we are too close to an activity, tradition, mindset, we are often blind to a lot of the integral details that make it what it is.

For instance, I have learned along the way that white people seem to enjoy long conversations at the dinner table centered around furniture and home renovation. Please stab me with a spoon now. Make it stop. These conversations are mind-numbingly boring, and I don't beam with pride at my Caucasian ancestry when I find myself subjected to one. I've also learned that Trader Joe's is exceedingly white. I mean, luckily I always see a beautifully diverse staff when I shop there, but it's definitely marketed to white people. I can't really tell you how I know this, it's just something you pinpoint after stepping back from your own culture and living in the midst of another.

When Lefty and I are at a fundraiser for our local Buddhist temple, or at a Lao wedding, I look around and find that I am either the only white person in a crowd of a couple hundred or one of about three who have a skin tone like mine. At first when I started dating him, I worried if it was disrespectful for me to attend certain events with him. But, while I'm aware that I may do or say something at times that is unintentionally inappropriate, Lefty's Lao community is accepting of me and I appreciate them all so much. Some of the most friendly and generous people I've ever encountered. I'm exceedingly attached to each and every one of them, and I learn so much by watching their respect for their elders, love of their children and incredible knack for never, ever taking a bad picture at gatherings. I've studied this photo op topic, but half the time I still find myself being that girl with the funny stance or nervous expression on her face, while all the women around me look like supermodels. To be clear, I am not trying to further the stereotypes of Asian women only being seen as sex objects. That is a sick viewpoint far too pervasive in our society. I'm simply acknowledging our huge amount of insanely beautiful friends. But they are not ONLY beautiful. They are strong, intelligent, multifaceted women I am honored to know.

When Lefty and I first got together, I felt insecure. At parties the Lao women around me were all so perfect I started wondering, "Why is he with me?" Don't get me wrong, I've always been a beautiful woman, and even in the midst of my weight struggles (the struggle is real!) I don't doubt my beauty, but I guess I'd say it's an imperfect, unusual kind of beauty. Whereas, most of the women in our circle have every hair in place at all times and appear as if they have a personal stylist and makeup artist tucked in their back pocket. That's not me. I've tried to make it me, but I always fail. I actually get uncomfortable when I try to make my appearance overly flawless. I think I like being a bit flawed. It reminds me that I'm real and imperfect, and I'm allowed to love myself anyway. Imperfections and all.

An interesting lesson about Lao customs is that it can be disrespectful to call people by their real names. I believe this rule applies only if the person you are addressing is older than you are. It's best to address those older than oneself with terms like "Uncle," "Aunt," "Sis," "Brother," you get the idea. I can't imagine what my mother-in-law thought of me when I was learning this rule. Lefty broke it to me one night that I should be careful not to call his mom by her name. I had no idea. I explained to him that in white culture it's just the opposite. Learning, remembering, then pronouncing someone's name properly the next time you see them is a sign of respect. It means that you paid attention when you first met them. It tells them they meant something to you, enough for you to call them by their name.

Not so for Laotian culture. Also, when walking by an elder, it is very important to crouch down and bow so you are lower than they are as you pass. I have been an utter failure at this. I finally know this rule, but I can't seem to remember to put it in play at the pertinent time. I'm working on it. And I'm getting better.

There is an elder in the community whom I adore so much. She has the most wonderful smile. Even though we have a language barrier, and I never can understand what she is saying to me, I feel and hope I'm right about our having a strong, loving bond. There's just something about her. She's the mother of several friends of ours, grandmother to several more and, actually, great grandmother to some sweet little ones as well. I hope to goodness the next time I see this wise woman I will bow down sufficiently low to convey my sincere admiration. I want her to know how much I admire her.

Update: I saw the elder I spoke of at a party recently. And I finally *remembered* to bow down sufficiently as I addressed her. And guess what? She told me she *loved me!!!* I just about fainted with shock and happiness. I told her with great enthusiasm, "I love you, too!!"

There is a joyful and contagious quality to Lao culture. My husband's smile and laugh melt my heart and I never grow tired of them. He is the hardest working man I know. He's been a heavy equipment operator for Waste Management for well over a decade. He works long hours. Often six days a week, yet doesn't complain much. He has that Buddhist attitude about living in the present and focusing on gratitude. He's a good influence on me, because even though I know it's bad to get overly angry about things I can't control, I often find myself doing it anyway. On a daily basis, he leads by example about how to be a good person and soak up the sunshine of life.

I honestly feel more "normal" when surrounded by diversity. It's not really that I am ashamed of my heritage, but being white sometimes feels so bland. I'm okay with being who I am, but I feel the most at home when I am exposed to other cultures, new ways of looking at life, death and everything in between.

I never saw anything to like about Redding until I met Lefty, who showed me everything there was to love about it. Everything that doesn't meet the eye at first. The Southeast Asian community is tight-knit and dedicated to preserving its traditions and ways of life. They pass on their beautiful languages to their children and grandchildren and never forget the homelands from which they, or the generations before them, came. Sometimes I look at all the colorful clothing and smiling faces and I am overcome with emotion. I feel incredibly lucky to have found Lefty and to know and love his wonderful circle of family and friends.

Chapter 57

Anxiety

I'm tired of this sick feeling in my stomach. Like everything is wrong with the world in this moment. I've had anxiety all my life, you might think I'd be used to it by now, but I'm not. Some days I feel like I want to crawl out of my skin. It's this buzzing, panicky sensation that makes everything uneasy and complicated. Just keeping up with family appointments induces a type of bizarre stress I can't explain.

Does it have to be this hard? Was I born with some sort of genetic defect? I don't know. I feel a little guilty because I'm pretty sure I've passed down these tough traits to my daughters. But then again, they do have half their genetics from their father and he has not had it easy with mental health issues either. There we go. Gonna blame it on the dad and walk away. Phew…that was a close one.

Because I'm aware of my struggle with mental and emotional balance, I try not to assume the worst for my children, but I do talk to them often about how they are doing, and I'm a big proponent of counseling. Mental health struggles are nothing to keep secret. It becomes a stronger, more vicious monster when it's kept caged in the dark.

And do you ever notice that anxiety and fear tend to muffle intuition? It's as if, once fear has crept inside us, through an open upstairs window we could have sworn we closed, our ability to decipher between real and imagined danger slips away. The clouds that gather around fear momentarily block out the light of our psychic abilities.

I am aware that I need to clear my head before I try to tap into my higher senses. But knowing and doing are two different things, and often I fall short. I'm still learning, still trying and still seeking help. Always.

Chapter 58

I Want You to Know Me

Some people like to go through life holding back. Hiding. Masking how they really feel and concealing what they really think. That's not me. Someday when I die I want people to say, "Hey, I knew her." And I want them to mean it.

I don't want to be a mystery to unravel. I'd rather be an open book. An open book that risks offending or appearing overly plaintiff, but at least it's honest. I'd rather be the one who admits my stupid mistakes and doesn't cover my scars. Because other people can relate to that. We all make stupid mistakes and not one of us is getting out of this life alive. Scars are inevitable. Let yours not accrue in vain. Let the marks on your body, soul and heart teach you something. Dig deep and look hard. The lessons are there.

I wish we could live an entire lifetime without hurting anybody. But there is good and bad in everyone. Our task as individuals is to cultivate our good to the highest level possible and to evaluate our bad. Learn from it. Not suppress it, but try to turn it into something better. Kinder. Try to work through it without taking it out on other people.

I want you to know me. My good, my bad, and my ugly. But I also want you to know my beauty. Imperfect though it is. People can spend all day judging others, and believe me, I'm guilty of that more than I like to acknowledge, but in judging we forget to simply observe. In observing we learn. We get to *know.* I believe that most people have good intentions and good intentions count for a lot. Also, a well placed "sorry" goes a long way. Not all the way, but a long way.

To anyone reading this who has ever been upset with me, or felt wronged by my actions or words, this is my sorry to you. Hopefully I've already said it in person. It's not fun to have to apologize, but I make myself do it when I know I'm in the wrong. I don't want any unfinished business, and I don't want anyone to feel like I am okay with hurting people. Life is short and forgiveness is not my strong point. Never has been. But I do cultivate strength in the area of apologizing when it's warranted. Sometimes that is all we are seeking when we're hurt, right? Sorry is a magical word that can mean so much.

Chapter 59

Camping Is One of My Top Ten Fears

I hate camping. It's not a little type of hate, it's a big type of hate. It's an, "Okay, I want to leave right this second and we just got here," type of hate. I briefly did alright with it as a kid but quickly burned out. I don't like being dirty, I don't like the sun, and by the way, I don't tan, I *burn*. I go from white to lobster-red in as little as ten minutes of direct sunlight on my skin. Since I'm not a morning person, I can't stand waking up in a tent to bright daylight and thinking it must be 10 o'clock only to find that it's fucking 7:00 a.m.

Here's the deal: I've *tried* to like, or even love, camping. I *wish* I could love it. It would make life so much easier every summer. But loving camping is not happening for me. Not now, not tomorrow, not ever.

Maybe it's because I was raised in such a rustic environment that I felt almost like I was camping all the time even while at home. But I think really it's just my personality and there's no use fighting it. Here's a little tip for anyone in my life who wants to hang out with me while I'm in a good mood: DON'T TAKE ME CAMPING. You're welcome.

Chapter 60

I Needed to Hear That

At work today I was busy with phones ringing off the hook, drowning in cc'd emails, and a steady stream of students to help with tricky issues. Then one of my favorite students popped up in front of me at the desk. I was on my own while my co-workers were at lunch. We finished up the student's paperwork and then she leaned in and quietly told me something I'll never forget. She said, "Can I tell you a secret? Out of all the people here, you are my favorite."

I cannot express how much those words brought happy tears to my eyes. In a mostly thankless job, it's times like these that my heart smiles. And it wasn't that I needed to feel "better" than any of my co-workers. I love most of my co-workers, and they're wonderful at what they do. But I needed to feel needed and appreciated. And those feelings are few and far between inside these office walls.

Thank you, dear student, for making me feel, for a moment, like I was doing something right. Your sweet words meant more to me than you will ever know.

Chapter 61

Honeymoon

Lefty and I went to the Big Island of Hawaii for our honeymoon. With the kids. And with my mom and step-dad. We had wanted to take the kids on a memorable vacation for so long, so we decided we might as well just combine it all. Perhaps not the most romantic choice, but he and I find time for romance in the smallest pieces of the day. The way he kisses my hand when he tells me he loves me. The way I stare into his eyes when I want to see his soul.

Another reason we made it a family trip was because my mom offered to pay for our plane tickets and lodging while we were there. An incredibly generous offer I could not turn down. We stayed at a vacation rental high on the side of a hill owned by one of Mom's best friends. It was breathtaking. Not walking distance to the ocean, but overlooking it in a way that allowed great enjoyment coupled with peace of mind that we would not be awakened by a tsunami in the night.

Can you see the love between us? I can.

It was late September and it so happened Hawaii was experiencing a record-breaking, sweat-drenching heat wave from Hell. Those who know me know what a baby I am about the heat. Every summer, even where I live, I think of moving to Siberia. Or at least Montana. So this Hawaii heat floored me. I was bummed out that it hit so hard. I felt like a spoiled brat to be complaining in one of the most beautiful places on Earth. This type of extreme heat is so rare on the islands that there's no air conditioning, *anywhere.* It's simply not needed in normal conditions. This meant clothes soaked through within five minutes after showering, makeup melted off, and my spirits were pretty low most of the trip. I'm happy we made the journey. The memories are lovely, but I would be lying if I said I wasn't extremely eager to get home when our week came to an end.

On a brighter note, the vacation house was so gorgeous it was like a scene out of a movie. My favorite things were the outdoor baths and showers. It was like a dream to run a bath, sink deep into the water, and look up to watch the ferns and blooming flowers overhead. Neon green geckos everywhere made me feel like I was in a Disney film. I liked the little clicking sounds they made. Slightly creepy and predatory, but hey, I'm not a cockroach, so I had no need to worry. And I'm glad I didn't know about the giant stinging centipedes until just before we left. I didn't see any, but hearing about them and being warned about what to do if I saw one scarred me for life.

Grandparents were lifesavers in keeping the kids occupied when Lefty and I were too tired to do anything in the heat of the day. They took Chloë, Gwen, and Cameron on many fun excursions. I think one of their favorite places was a spot frequented by sea turtles. They came back with some great pictures. And swimming seemed to be the favorite pastime, for obvious reasons.

I'm a bit ashamed to say this, but Lefty and I only made it out to swim in the ocean once. But that one time was a pretty magical experience. What was not magical is how sticky you feel after crawling out of the salt water. It was worth it, though. And touching the water made me think of Naomi. It was the first time I touched the ocean water in Hawaii since she was dropped into it eighteen years earlier. I almost felt like it was a way to introduce her to Lefty. Is that weird? That's probably weird.

It was fun to venture through the tiny tourist towns and buy souvenirs. We brought home some cool trinkets. Most of which we gave away to friends and family, but one I kept. An amethyst ring with a silver band. I spotted it in a little jewelry and crystal shop and recognized that I had wanted one like it for years. It was way overpriced and I didn't care. The shop owner was nice and I felt good about supporting her livelihood. At one point she noticed Lefty looking at a crystal said to have healing properties. She asked him, "Do you have stress in your life?" And he replied, "Not since I met my wife."

It was my favorite moment from the entire trip. Worth all the sweaty clothes and the melted makeup. Worth the travel time in uncomfortable airplane seats. Time with Lefty is worth all the treasure on Earth. And it's nice to know that he values time with me the same way.

Chapter 62

Joy

Miss Joy is a firecracker. Actually, I take that back. Miss Joy is an entire fireworks show. The kind that might be seen lighting up the dark sky after a royal baby is born, or as a display over fancy desserts at an elaborate wedding. She will both charm the pants off you and shock the hell out of you during the very same sentence. She is rude, unapologetic, mean, darling, and, believe it or not, even loveable. The list of words to describe this old lady goes on and on. And when I use the term "old lady," I'm not putting her down or trying to slight her in any way. She really is an old lady. A sassy one at that. Joy has lived ninety years on this planet, and she's learned a thing or two about how to get under peoples' skin. In all the right, and all the wrong ways.

I met her at my workplace a couple years back. She is retired now, but up until recently she still came in to proctor tests for instructors who teach off sight and only see their students over the TV screen from their workstation. Joy would be there making damn sure no one cheated, talked, looked at her funny, breathed, you get the picture. Intimidating as hell, and she knows it. Her tiny body can't weigh more than eighty pounds, but those eighty pounds would fuck you up if you chose not to play your cards right.

Sometimes she still comes by the office to say hi, raise hell, keep things interesting, or to participate in a potluck party for a coworker. And when she comes calling, you can bet she flies in on her broomstick. Even *she* will tell you that. She'll ask you how you're doing and then cut you off with a cunning or crude reply before you can finish your response. Miss Joy is most comfortable when she is making others around her shift in their seats. Nervous about how best to deal with her. But there's no right answer when she comes to town. It's all Joy all the time, and don't you dare try to detract from her spotlight. 'Cause she runs the show.

Joy loved to say outlandish things when she answered her home phone. Her favorite was, "Hannah's whorehouse, how can I help you?" Yep. I'm still cracking up, yet oddly uncomfortable over that one. And I'm sure that was her exact objective.

The only time I ever got truly mad at this woman was when she called me a bitch in the break room. Loudly. Around others. One of them being my boss. She could've been one hundred and ten years old at the time, I still would have been mad. I told her, "Hey, now, that crosses the line. You can't call me that, Missy." Surprisingly, she never did it again. But that's not to say she's gone soft.

The only thing soft about Miss Joy is her love for kittens. She's a crazy cat lady and I love her for it. I hear she just keeps accumulating more and more, because word spread about her big heart for homeless cats and people drop them at her doorstep.

Joy also has a big heart for homeless people and volunteers at the local soup kitchen in her area. She's not ready to sit back and relax in her old age. She's ready to kick ass and take names. And I'm ninety-nine percent positive that I've actually heard her speak that exact phrase on multiple occasions. Heck, with the way she talks on a daily basis, in public, she makes even my bad words in private or on paper sound like lines out of Mary Poppins.

Chapter 63

Shopping with Gwen

My favorite way to bond with Gwen is grocery shopping. Sounds mundane, right? But no, we have a ball the entire time. Smelling candles, laughing at the absurdity of some of the products on the shelf, and generally prancing down the aisles like we haven't a care in the world. Come to think of it, this activity seems to help our anxious minds calm down and just focus on the task at hand for a while.

Gwen and I went on one of these excursions yesterday. To our favorite store with everything under the sun. We strolled in with five items in mind and we walked out with at least fifty. And in the process we spotted all kinds of things we never knew we needed but just had to have. She picked out a yummy coffee scented candle for her room. It helps her forget she still has the guinea pig cage in her living quarters. Our little fur balls, Marvin and Reubin, are real handfuls, but we love them. However, we don't love how quickly their cage smells like a petting zoo. The candle will fix it, even if momentarily.

Gwen sure makes me laugh!

Gwen spotted small cans of cold brew coffee only ten calories each. We both gave a look of disgust, because we knew how bad they must taste. I said they should come with a simple warning that states: "Tastes like shit!" And she agreed with a laugh. I became excited when I actually remembered to get beets while in the produce section. I love beets yet only think to buy them about twice a year. It's a travesty. Steamed, boiled or sauteed beets taste like life to me. As if they hold within them the fountain of youth and the cure for cancer wrapped into one. I remember my mother making borscht when I was a small child. A Polish style beet soup, this concoction was divine and memorable. Comforting and earthy, with a richness of our Eastern European heritage simmered right into the deep red broth.

In the pet section we needed food pellets for the guineas, and we couldn't pass up getting them a couple kinds of treats as well. We were so excited to give them each some when we got home. Gwen opened the bag of small things that looked like orange chocolate chips and dropped two into the cage. Both piggies rushed over to smell them then glanced up at us as if to say, "What the fuck is this?" They looked offended, to be honest. That was $3.59 I should not have spent. But hey, maybe I can feed them to a neighbor dog or stray cat. The treats, that is, not the pets. If I were to try, would the cats and dogs also look up at me with such disdain in their accusing little eyes? Maybe. But I can handle it.

Towards the end of our grocery excursion I remembered we needed bread. I was strolling around looking for the bread isle when Gwen bluntly let me know that I do that every time we are there. I forget that there is no bread isle. Instead there is an entire *wall of bread* located opposite the checkout lines. Let me tell you, this store does not discriminate against its carbs. They honor them with this wall that seems to double as a shrine. You go near it and the sound of singing angels softly caresses your ears. And after choosing two different kinds of beautiful gluten-filled loaves, the angels whispered something else: "You are out of butter." Thank God for lovely little food angels. Gwen and I headed to the dairy section immediately. In that moment, all was well in our world.

Chapter 64

Is This What Caused My Weirdness?

I was five years old with my parents at a Vipassana meditation center. I can't remember whether we were all staying there during a ten-day meditation course or if I went with one parent to pick up the other. But what I do remember is being a very little girl who had climbed up to the top of a very large rock on the meditation center grounds. I think I was playing with other kids up there, or perhaps I was just being a loner and wanted a better vantage point for my observational activities. Regardless, I recall leaning over to look down at the ground from my high-up perch. I was like a sailor keeping watch in the crow's nest of a ship. I peeked down and the next thing I knew, I was on the ground. Face first. There must have been a live oak tree nearby, because I remember removing prickly dry leaves from my damaged forehead. A forehead that would soon develop an absolutely enormous goose egg. Painful and swollen.

The bump on my head was bad enough to alarm my parents, who tracked down a doctor at the center. I was shy and didn't want him to look at me, so I hid under a blanket. Eventually he coaxed me out, checked my forehead and shined a bright light in my eyes. Probably to check for a concussion. I look back now and I swear I must have had one. In fact, years later my best friend's mom attests that I had a major seizure when I stayed the night with them. I don't remember a thing, but I have always wondered what my brain would look like if I were to undergo an MRI. The image might be a bit more interesting than I would like.

Who knows? Maybe I have some brain damage like my daughter Chloë. She's awesome, so I would still be awesome, too. If I ever fall off a huge rock again, I will bite the bullet and get a more in-depth checkup for my noggin. But I'm okay with going to my grave never knowing what the inside of my brain looks like. Looking at what's inside my skull is not any sort of thing on my bucket list. I have far more important things to think about. Like, did I remember to put the ice cream back in the freezer after serving myself a larger than reasonable amount? And, will I get to the end of my life someday and look back, thinking to myself, "I should have eaten *more* ice cream, god damn it!"?

Chapter 65

Naomi's Jewelry Box

While sorting through some things from my garage today, I came across my sister's old jewelry box. A small creation made of wood. Our grandpa George gave us matching ones when we were kids. I opened hers and saw the little hair clips she used to wear. They have tiny dried flowers encased in glass. Pretty and perfect.

I loved Naomi's hair. When she was a teenager she often put it in flawless French braids. She reminded me of "Anne of Green Gables," the Megan Follows version. Those are the ones we grew up watching. My favorite movies of all time. "Anne of Green Gables" and the sequel, "Anne of Avonlea." I escaped into those lifelike films as a child and when the credits rolled, a little piece of me stayed in Anne's world.

To me, Naomi was Anne. She was stubborn, strong willed, easy to anger, and loved with all her heart. She held romantic views about life and was often disappointed when her fantasies didn't glow in the dim light of day as they did the night before in her dreams. I think I have that inside me, too. I always want more than people say I should want. I expect better than what some try to tell me I deserve. Not to say it's exactly an entitlement complex. Some may see it that way. But to me it's

---

Sweet sixteen year old Naomi, in India.

more like a deep knowing that life can be more glorious than a lot of us let ourselves believe.

Majestic Naomi at the "Palace of the Winds."

The only thing that killed me about the Anne story was that Matthew had to die. That scene on the green hillside, working the cattle when he collapsed. I will never forget the first time I saw it. I was at home in the cabin, and I just about died myself, right there on the couch. It was too much tragedy for my small heart to handle. Watching Anne cradle the man who had taken her in and cherished her so dearly. Hearing him tell her that it was always her he wanted in his life. Not a boy, like he was supposed to pick up that day at the train station. It was always her.

I was born without the mechanism to shelter myself from pain. I am incapable of protecting myself from it. I sometimes observe people who maintain a type of stoic nature that helps them keep a distance between themselves and the things that rip them to shreds. That is not an option for me. Pain books a one-night stay in my soul and doesn't check out for a lifetime. I can't evict it even if I try. So I strive to be patient with myself. Patient with the pain. Since I know it is never-ending, I don't waste energy trying to chase it away.

Like Naomi and Anne, I'm just making my way through life trying to see the beauty in all things. Yes, it's painful. And yes, the pain is worth it.

Chapter 66

Blue Wall

Last weekend our new landlord sent a handyman to our house. He was there to take down the wallpaper paneling on one of the walls in our living room. I'm still at a loss why our landlord felt this was necessary right now, but it's not up to me.

Anyway, I was nervous about what they'd find when the paneling came down. The only reason I could think of for it going up in the first place was that the wall underneath must be badly damaged. Lefty thought maybe our landlord believed his father hid money in the wall before he died. Our daughter, Chloë, said she hoped there weren't dead bodies behind it. That idea really got to me and I began to wish that the landlord would rethink his plans and leave things be until we moved out, or until he finally decided to sell us the house.

The guy worked away on our wall, and I wondered more feverishly what the take down would reveal. Finally, I heard him call to Lefty and me that he was finished. I came down the hallway and heard him say, "Well, I hope you like blue." I looked over at the uncovered wall. It was a mess of picture-hanging holes, dust and dirt, with a soft blue paint that could use some serious redoing. I was horrified. I mean, I hadn't really liked that one oddball wall of flowery wallpaper but, it was in fairly good shape and at least blended with the other solid white paint in the house. Now, here was this uninvited artistic touch that had been abused by countless renters before us. Looking like no one on earth had heard of spackle. I pictured doing that part myself, but knowing my luck, when it came to painting over the spackled areas, I would go to a home store and come back with thirty shades of blue and none of them would be the matching one I needed.

Right now I'm sitting on my couch looking at said wall. Wondering what kind of stories it would tell if it could talk. I'm relieved it does not seem to be hiding any tales of murders from days gone by. I wouldn't have been opposed to finding bundles of cash, but technically it wouldn't have belonged to us anyway. That would be quite a letdown. I'm curious about who the person was that picked out this particular shade of blue and why they were drawn to it. Mysteries like this bug me when I am well aware I will never be given the answers.

I wiped down the blue wall the day it was revealed. It didn't make it look any less dirty from dust build up, but at least it didn't creep me out as much, knowing it was clean. Our landlord plans to install a central heating and cooling system soon, and I'm worried about when he will raise our rent to pay for his renovations. I think the one perk to renting is the fact that you are not responsible for home improvements and repairs. But most homeowners who rent their places out find ways to pass along improvement costs to their tenants. When that time comes, I suppose Lefty and I will decide whether we will stand for it, or whether we will start looking for another house to live in.

This one already has a lot of quirky qualities. Like electrical outlets that smoke when the power comes back on from an outage, and spots under the carpet that feel like they might be rotting away. Needless to say, this is not our dream home. But it's our home for now and it keeps us from being out in the cold. We *really* miss our original landlord who passed away. He made the quirks less aggravating because he was so darn sweet. He made the annoying aspects of this place tolerable. Now that he's gone I'm starting to see more of the grunge, and it's bothering me. But it's all okay. Even the stupid blue wall. It's okay, too. Not what I want, but we are not out on the streets having to sleep under bridges and beg for food. Compared to so many unfortunate souls we are rich. And I don't ever want to lose sight of how lucky we really are.

Chapter 67

Not a Morning Person

I don't trust morning people. If you're one of them, I'm sorry to offend you. For me, mornings are meant for sleeping. Waking up is allowed around 10:00 a.m. or later. When I get up for work after hearing my alarm go off, I feel this type of horrible despair. How dare the workaday world interrupt my delicate sleep patterns. Fuck that.

I often hear people say I will get used to getting up early. They're lying. Getting up at 10:00 a.m. and going to sleep after midnight is my dream schedule. Sleeping till 12 noon is even better. That's one of the reasons I like performing so much. That's exactly what I get to do on days I have a show. It suits me.

Last summer I stupidly agreed to start work a full two hours earlier than the norm for six weeks. It was miserable. We even got Fridays off during that time and it still didn't make it okay. It was quite an eye-opener. I realized that it is really true—I'd rather have to work five days a week if it means I can sleep in a little bit more during weekday mornings.

I firmly believe that whoever came up with the standard American work schedule is a sadistic bastard who was fully aware of the suffering he would cause when he put it into play. Not cool, man. Not cool.

Chapter 68

Death

Death has been on my mind a bit too much lately. It's one factor that makes me wonder about how depressed I may or may not be. I'm not a psychiatrist, so I can't exactly diagnose myself, but when I find I'm thinking more about the eventual death of every living thing and less about the excitement of living this beautiful life, that's my red flag that I'm not feeling well. It's quite a balance, right? Being realistic about the human life cycle while trying to attach to this life and live it with courage and enthusiasm. It's *hard.*

When I was growing up I had this fear that flashed through my head. My mind would go black, as if a dark curtain was suddenly hung in front of it to block out the light. I realized in horror, anew each time, that I was going to die someday. My parents and siblings were *going to die someday.* I can still vividly feel the gripping terror when I think back. And the way I got through it was to push it out of my thoughts as best I could, move along with my day, and pretend that the demise of our physical bodies would never come to pass. I was pretty much able to keep pretending this until one of us *did* die. When my sister passed away it was so hard to reconcile. It wasn't fair, it wasn't anything I ever expected to happen, at least not until many decades down the road, especially at her young age of twenty-four. It made that black curtain in my mind feel anchored in reality and cruel.

Even today I can't seem to put on a brave face when staring at death. I know that everything and everyone who is born will eventually die, and that inescapable thought should comfort me, perhaps. Strength in numbers. It's not like it's only going to happen to me and my family.

The one time I can kind of come to grips with it is when the loved one passing away is around ninety years old. It's still hard, but I can take some comfort in knowing that they led a long, natural life and it was truly their time to go. But as I get a little older, I have a new terrible black curtain drape over me from time to time. My parents just turned seventy. I don't want to think about the possibility of only having them in my life another twenty years. That's horrifying and the thought keeps me up at night. For all I know maybe they'll both live to be one hundred and ten. It could happen, but still, I find myself wrestling too often with thoughts of finality that I don't want to entertain.

I think losing Naomi early in my life scarred me so deeply that I look at all death as bad. As something inherently evil in some way. But how could this be? If life is such a beautiful gift, and every life ends at some point in time, does that mean every life is ushered away by some type of evil spirit for an evil purpose? Of course not. That doesn't even make sense to my own jaded and overly worried logic. I just feel the grief from losing my sister so damn much, and so damn often that it feels like a river with a strong current I am stuck in for all eternity. The thought of losing someone else extremely close to me is simply too unbearable. It will encroach uninvited in dark times and seize me with fear. It's as if I reached my quota of grief with my sister, and now I'm saying, "No more!" to the universe. Foolishly thinking that the universe can protect me from one of the fundamental human experiences of existence.

I just wish I could find more meaning in death, and more ways to accept it and feel that it is not all bad. It's my rebellious nature, it seems, that keeps me pushing against all things I don't like. And I really don't like pain, grief, and saying goodbye.

Some people might recommend religion to me. Maybe as a way to explain the unexplainable and find comfort in the confines of ancient scripture. But I'm too much of a realist to believe in an actual heaven or hell. I believe in aspects of those here on earth. But not the ones above and below us constructed to make human beings behave a certain way. For me it's more of a personal spiritual journey toward finding ways of living my life un-encompassed by dread.

I am so attached to life. I have so many things I want to get done, and I'm acutely aware that we are all born into this world without enough time. So we make do with what we've got. We make the moments count and we count our blessings often. In most respects, I'm still ok with pushing that dark curtain aside when it comes over me, and finding more ways to live joyfully, creatively, with purpose. Because it comes down to the fact that death will come for us all, but we die while still alive if we let it run the show while our lungs are still breathing.

Chapter 69

Depression

After writing all about death I figure you might need me to lighten the mood for you now. I gotch you! Let's talk about DEPRESSION!! I mean, hey, if we're aware we're suffering from it that means at least we're still alive, right?? Maybe this year will be the year I finally get on meds. Would antidepressants help me stomach my desk job? If they did, would that ultimately be a positive or a negative? Most days I have a hard time even wanting to get in the shower. I'm constantly coaching myself with words like: "Come on, Arianna, be thankful for all the good in your life." "Be appreciative that you have a body to wash." "You're alive…LIVE."

But maybe this is what depression is. You see so clearly your flawed thinking and wasted time feeling blue and resentful of everyday tasks, yet you can't drag yourself up into the light. If you could do it easily, wouldn't depression be nonexistent? It runs in my family. My dad has dealt with it for years. I'm happy he finally decided to get on antidepressants. It may not be the answer for everyone, but for those they can help, I say more power to 'em.

I had actually been feelinging pretty darn great recently. Losing a bit of weight, working on a new album, writing more songs, got a raise in my last paycheck. The list goes on. Yet, out of the blue, out of freaking nowhere, I started feeling completely depressed today. Like *really* bad. It's a little scary how quickly you can go from manically awesome to tragically sad and hopeless. I can't stand this about depression. It pisses me off and I will try to do everything in my power to not go down with the ship for too long. I've come too far.

Update: (Approximately six months later) I have gained back all ten pounds. I have been struggling even more intensely with depression and anxiety, and at the end of my last counseling appointment, my counselor actually *suggested* I try a low-dose antidepressant. My doctor's appointment is scheduled for a week and a half from now. I'm pinning a lot of hopes on this appointment. I do know I need help.

Update: I went to that appointment yesterday, met my new doctor, he was awesome! He didn't rush me out of the room, didn't make me feel silly for asking questions, listened to my concerns, ordered blood work and prescribed the antidepressant Wellbutrin. I am ready to start a new chapter in my life. I AM READY!

Update: (Two months later) I'm experiencing wonderful relief from the intense body exhaustion I have suffered most of my life. That is a very welcome effect from this pharmaceutical I'm trying out.

On the flip side, it is not helping in any way with my job. Nope. Nada. Zip. I am still demoralizingly unhappy at my office every day. And I do mean every day. So much so that the other day I had to meet with my boss about an ongoing project, and when she asked me how I was doing, I immediately broke down crying. Thankfully, she is kind and understanding, but nonetheless, it's not at the top of my list to break down when faced with a question as simple as, "How are you doing?"

And to elaborate a bit more for honesty's sake, a little later on the very same workday, my *top* boss, I'll call him Aiden, just happened to stop in the break room while I was on lunch break. Wanna guess what Aiden asked? Wanna take a wild fucking guess?? Yes, he asked me, "*How are you doing?*" And let me tell you, he almost NEVER asks me that. Although he is a nice guy, he usually doesn't have time to even acknowledge I *exist,* much less to check on my current well-being. Any guesses how I reacted to his question? You're right. I broke down in tears...again. Embarrassing!!! I think I really shook him up. He's a sweet man when speaking with him one on one, but my overly open emotions appeared to be a bit much for him.

To his credit, though, he took me outside to talk a bit more, and pointed me in the direction of an onsite counselor who happened to be on campus that day. The counselor was helpful. Guess what I did when I first started talking to her? Yep. She handed me the tissue box within one tenth of a second. Apparently crying is my signature move in a professional work environment. Can you get paid for being a professional cryer? If so, what am I waiting for? Sign me the fuck up!

Chapter 70

The Best of Intentions

I swear, sometimes I experience something that shakes up my bleeding heart and I start to wonder, *Why do I even try?* The origin of my musings is this: The other day my husband brought home a couple small crayfish, or crawdads? I don't even know the difference. *Is* there a difference? Anyway, he had used some for bait while fishing with friends at the lake. I spotted them in a tupperware container of water with some fresh leafy greens sprinkled on top for the little critters to hide under and nibble on. I felt a bit sick to my stomach when I realized why these small things were off in a corner of our dark garage. They were destined to be on a hook waiting to be eaten by an unlucky fish. So, when Lefty got home from work I casually mentioned that I found his crayfish and gave them a top-off of cold water in their container. And I added, "If they stick around too much longer I'm gonna want to keep them for pets." He laughed and said they could live out their lives in a fish bowl on the table if I wanted to make it happen. I liked this idea!

The next day I tracked down the stored fish bowl we had from way back when, during my girls' beta fish phase. I can't tell you how many beta funerals we conducted over the years. Complete with fresh flowers laid alongside the body and somber words recited with the heartfelt emotion that any dead beta deserves. As I spotted the bowl way back behind some forgotten dishes in a cabinet, a smile flashed across my face. We were in business. Pet crayfish business, to be exact. I filled the bowl with water, Lefty transferred the critters, and we both had fun putting a few decorative rocks and shells at the bottom. Also fresh greens for the pair to chew on.

Everything was going great for the duo the next day. I did get nervous that they were not getting enough to eat, so I looked up what to feed them in addition to their greens. One google post suggested carrot for a treat. I got out my smallest grater and shredded a small amount of carrot into the fish bowl. After a little while I could see one of the crayfish eating the bright orange pieces and he seemed to be enjoying them.

Now let's fast forward *one more day.* I was running around getting ready for a songwriting session when I glanced at the fishbowl. Aware I would need to change the water soon. Surprised it was already murky. Then with horror I spotted it. At the bottom of the bowl. A headless crayfish. I felt like I just stumbled upon a murder scene. Even wondered if I should snap a picture to show to Lefty, in case by the time he got home all evidence was gone. In case the still-living crayfish decided he was snacky and finished dining on his cannibalized friend.

Wow, I thought, *Way to go, Arianna. You wanted to 'save the crayfish' and now look what happened?!* I felt a little silly. And I'd be lying if I said my compassion for the remaining little guy hadn't diminished. It had diminished a lot. I mean, I wasn't about to throw water on to boil and cook the little sucker, but *damn*. All of a sudden he seemed like he had an evil look in his eye and I wondered what ruthless plans he would hatch next.

Moral of the story? Don't assume each time you try to do something nice for other living things that they will understand your motive and reward you with pristine behavior. Sometimes they will flip us their middle finger with their crayfish claw and kill their roomate. In cold blood. And there's simply nothing we can do about it.

Chapter 71

Harper

We had a few classes together. She was in my grade in high school. I remember her great laugh. Full of mischief. She had a big personality and was known for being a loudmouth and class clown. Over time I noticed she was paying more attention to me than the norm. Making a point to tease me flirtatiously in class, giving me tight hugs in the hallway. I experienced something I'd never felt before. I was falling in love with a girl. That was utterly surprising and new to me.

Harper was so masculine that she exuded almost all male energy. Especially after she cut her dark brown hair short. She looked so good. My head was spinning with questions about how I could be, to my knowledge, straight, but also head over heels for this boyish classmate of mine. I loved the attention she gave me. She made me feel seen, beautiful and valued. Ironically, though, I only realized later on that she was playing me just like a guy might. She already had a girlfriend, a model a year older who had moved up from L.A. And Harper didn't feel it was pertinent information. But I was never all that mad at her for walking into my life and stirring things up. She was near impossible to stay angry with.

We found ourselves making out at parties. Hiding out on the back porch of our friend's house where no one could see us. There was something intoxicating about her. I've always been guilty of falling in love too fast. I've let myself get hurt so many times. But really, it came down to sleeping over with Harper one night and she wanted to have sex with me. I had never had sex with anyone at that point. And that was when I was finally putting the pieces together that she had that on-and-off-again girlfriend. So I told her no. I could sleep with her in her bed. I still wanted to be close to her. But I was not going to let her have sex with me.

It was confusing. How could I feel so in love with Harper and at the same time feel like sex just wouldn't work? Regardless of her girlfriend or no girlfriend status at the time. Looking back, I always come to the same conclusion. She wasn't a guy. I was deeply attracted to her. Had a huge place in my heart for her. But she wasn't a guy. It certainly wasn't that I felt it would be wrong for us to have a sexual relationship if I felt so inclined. I was raised to be very open-minded about LGBTQ rights. And more than that, I had numerous gay friends and family members whom I cared about tremendously. I came to the conclusion that perhaps in this case I was slightly wired to be bisexual, but only in terms of attractions. Actual sex? Apparently not.

I think about Harper often. I'd love to know how she's doing. Haven't seen her in over twenty years. I hope she's living a joyous and happy life wherever she is. She gave me a gift of a different kind of emotional connection than I'd ever experienced with another human being. She allowed me to learn things about myself I didn't know before. I'm thankful for her mischief in my life for that brief moment in time.

Chapter 72

For a Reason

Out of the blue, I woke up with too many negative thoughts today. We all want to think we are here for a reason. That we were born for a reason. That we have some divine purpose for existing here on Earth. But what if we are wrong? What if that's just a lie we tell ourselves so that we can survive each day? What if nothing has a purpose? What if we are born, we die, and nothing in between matters? How fucking terrifying would that be?

These are the thoughts that are consuming me today. I'm worried. Worried that maybe I've spent my whole life striving for a type of grand success and glory that was never meant to be mine. What if this book never gets published? What if I never find a literary agent who will take a risk and take me on? What if I never get around to making a second album or landing a songwriting publishing deal? What if, what if, what if…

When I get tired of trying to be strong and positive with my thoughts and intentions, this is the swamp where I end up. I wade through the muck without even a pair of rain boots. Just bare feet covered in swampiness and scared of being bitten by unknown aquatic creatures with teeth. My feet try to close eyes they don't have, so they won't have to watch through the murkiness as harmful beings slither close. The swamp that is my uncontrollably anxious mind is teaming with danger and all I want to feel, all I desperately want to feel, is safe.

Chapter 73

An Unexpected Visitor (Or, Damn! Wish I'd Been Wearing My Glasses!!)

A loud, aggressive knock woke me out of a dead sleep. I looked at the clock. It was 7:02 a.m. I got out of bed and quickly walked to the door. "Who is it?" I asked. An odd silence answered back, so I walked to a window where I could peek through the blinds. I saw a teenage boy standing at the door, bundled in a bulky warm jacket and winter hat. He knocked again, very loudly. I asked again, "Who is it?" Yet again he did not answer me back explaining his presence. My confusion was growing rapidly. I tiptoed over to the window again and peeked out. The young man was now sitting on my doorstep making a phone call, and I could distinctly overhear him say to the person on the other end of the line, "Yeah, I think it's the wrong house." At this point I was becoming genuinely freaked out. Another knock rang out sharp in the cold morning air. My patience was out, I was super scared, and I yelled back, "Who the FUCK is it??! I'm calling the cops!"

Now, here's the part in the story where it becomes very uncomfortable, because long story short, it turns out that the "boy" at the door was actually a former middle school teacher of my daughter, Gwen's. Yep, the "boy" was a grown woman named Ms. Geller. And if I had thought to throw on my glasses as I peeked through the window, I would have caught on. Because Ms. Geller does not look like a boy at all. She is a beautiful woman, I am simply blind without corrective lenses. Another thing that could have helped tip me off before I made the unfortunate decision to cuss out a very nice, *very* Christian, mentor of my daughter's, would have been if Gwen had been awake and running around getting ready for this said teacher to pick her up for the breakfast they were going to with another fellow teacher and Gwen's best friend, Nhu. But miss Gwen had overslept, didn't hear her alarm, and when I realized that the person on the other side of the door mumbled something about thinking that Gwen lived there before they drove off, I immediately ran to her bedroom and asked her if she had been expecting someone this early in the morning. She jumped up saying, “Oh my God! Oh my God!! Yes. Ms. Geller and Mr. Pearson were gonna pick me up for breakfast! I overslept!!”

I had the lovely task of explaining to my fifteen year old daughter that I had just yelled an obscenity at her favorite female teacher, and from here on out she will always think of Gwen as “that girl with the crazy mom.”

Gwen did in fact get picked up after the confusion cleared, and I asked her to profusely apologize to Ms. Geller. Gwen swears that once she and Nhu were in the car with her they all had a good laugh about the whole thing. I’m just aware I have poisoned my image beyond repair with a certain middle school teacher, and now I assume she thinks Gwen needs Sunday school more than ever. And I have a strong feeling she’ll plan an impromptu exorcism next time she finds herself knocking on my door. Hell, with what I said, I wouldn’t blame her.

Chapter 74

Burned Out on Parenting

This is not going to be a glowing chapter about my children. Yes, I love them. Yes, I could not live without them. No, I wouldn't mind if miraculously I could be off of mommy duty for a couple months. I naively thought the exhaustion factor would stop some day. I'm eighteen-plus years into this journey and it's still *hard.*

I still get woken up when I try to nap, I still get fussed at when they're hungry. Luckily they're potty trained, but not much else has changed. My irritations and impatience are not their fault, I just don't know how other mothers do it. How they never have a cross word with their kids. Never raise their voice. I'm normally a pretty nice person, but as a parent, when I get overdone I'm not always that nice. I never learned what it was like to be a full adult before I had to take care of children. I know that's part of my problem.

Having kids so young put me in a state of feeling like I'm never in control of my own life. It induced a sense of powerlessness I've never really been able to shake. It's odd to me that my biggest blessings in life are also my biggest challenges. But I'm guessing that parenting is not easy for anyone. Even those who carefully planned out their whole lives and had their first kid at thirty. I just wonder if people like that feel more control over their circumstances than I do. I guess I'll never know.

Today has not been fun. And I'm sure it also does not help that we are having our third full day of no power from a crazy storm. It knocked out power to most of our city, downed hundreds of trees, and has put me in one of the worst moods I've had to battle in a couple years. You know that feeling when you try to be strong, you try to stay positive, and then there comes a distinct moment when you give up on both? I have food rotting in our refrigerators and freezers due to this electrical situation. I have no will to even get in the shower, yet have to be at a gathering for a loved one who died in a bit.

I admit it. I'm a wreck. A self-centered, uncontrolled wreck of a woman, wife, and mother right now. And this is me *on antidepressants.* They don't make every day great, but they do make my life better. Today I'm experiencing the part about how they don't make every day great. This too shall pass...I hope.

Chapter 75

Little Ones

At work today, a student brought in her almost one-year-old little boy. He was INSANELY cute!!! I smiled at him, he smiled at me and my heart melted. His mom said with a laugh, "He has a thing for blondes."

And speaking of little ones, let's talk about the newest member of our family. Little Miss Gianna Grace. Our baby niece. She's been such a blessing and welcome addition to our family on Lefty's side. Seven months old going on twenty five. She's a sassy pants and a half, I tell you! A sassy pants who did NOT like being left at our house by her parents on New Years Eve. We got the text from her beautiful mama around 7:00 p.m. She asked if we were busy, and if we could watch the baby from 8:00 to 11:00 that night. Lefty and I were both feeling antisocial and really only wanted to be around each other, not out in a crowd for the festive evening. So, we said, "Sure! We would love to babysit Gigi!"

Gianna and Uncle Lefty watering the yard.

The baby arrived in her car seat, and the crying began the second I tried to take her out of it. She was not impressed with anyone picking her up who was not her mom. I don't blame her. Lefty and I took turns walking her up and down the hallway. He showed her our pet guinea pigs, thinking they could cheer her up. She was scared of them and they were scared of her, so that was a well-meant but failed attempt to stop the ear-piercing screams coming from this little house guest of ours.

I found some stuffed animal toys from our daughters' room. I thought, "These are bound to distract her and cheer her up!" Nope. She seemed even more angry when I offered them to her. She appeared almost offended I would present such things to her when she was in such a fragile emotional state. Her little frown is impressive. It takes you down. Like, waaay down. Little miss sassy pants just kept crying, screaming, and frowning away. Lefty and I felt like brand new parents all over again.

This ordeal went on for a good two hours. And just as we were both becoming a bit discouraged at our lack of skills to calm the little cutie, and as her screams seemed to get gradually louder than before, my husband whispered in my ear: "Let's have another..."

I about died laughing. We shared a great big belly laugh over the fact that that thought seemed so absurd in that moment. I'm glad we're on the same page. No going back to the new baby stage! No way. But we do LOVE Miss Gigi! Even when she doesn't love us.

Chapter 76

Into the Darkness

I'm struggling hard with the dark this winter. Even my medication does not lift the depression right now. I'll be doing alright during the light of day and then, boom! The sun sets and I feel trapped in a dark box and it's as if my every dream and aspiration has been ripped away and I now exist for no purpose whatsoever except to suffer claustrophobia and dread. It happens every year, but it never gets easier. My skin crawls and I feel completely unsettled. I think I know why animals hibernate. I'm gonna go throw on some PJs and I'll see you again in two to three months...

Chapter 77

Fuck Is My Favorite Word

(I almost made this the title of the book. LOL)

Today I had a pre-op appointment for a hysterectomy I'm having in a week. I've been anemic for months even while taking an iron supplement, and my OBGYN approved yanking my uterus out through my belly button. Or wait, is it coming out through my vagina? Regardless, sounds fun, right? At least I'll be asleep while she does it. And she'll be assisted by a robot, so that's kind of cool. I assume if someone were to take a snapshot of the procedure and show it to people out of context it would look like I am the victim of an alien abduction. So...that's kind of cool, too. Or scary? Disturbing? I don't know and I don't care. Just get this thing that is draining my entire body's blood supply out of me, please.

This is still the year 2020 and age of the pandemic, so my appointment included a covid19 test. I was slightly nervous but I figured it couldn't be all that bad. I mean millions of people have had them, right? In other countries. I think here in the U.S. they've officially tested about five people and I can now proudly say that I am one of them. Anyway, my pre-op nurse was the sweetest woman. I couldn't see her face under the mask, but I would venture to guess she was mid to late fifties. With the voice of a sweet, southern little girl.

As she explained what the test would entail I got more worried than I already was. She said it would feel like I fell overboard in the ocean and got salt water up my nose. I hoped she was exaggerating, but I thanked her for the fair warning. She proceeded to open the swab and stick it up my left nostril until it felt like it was piercing my eye and protruding through my skull. I mean, JESUS! It fucking hurt like hell!! When it was done I kept expecting to start recovering from the discomfort. Instead I was sick to my stomach and light headed. My nose hurt like crazy, my eyes watered and I had to lay my head on the desk in front of me. Then even that tactic wasn't cutting it. I told the nurse I felt like I was going to pass out. Instead of waiting to find out while I fell to the floor, I pulled the chair next to mine close and sprawled my body over both seats as best I could. Lying haphazardly on my back all I could think was, *What the fuck just happened?!* This trauma response my body was running with really took me by surprise. I realized I had been cussing out loud quite a bit, both during and after the actual administration of the test. So I apologized to the nurse for my bad language. And she replied, "Oh honey, no need to say sorry. Fuck is my favorite word!" Then she added, in that sweet southern voice of hers, "And my favorite *saying* is "for fuck's *sake!*" She is officially my favorite nurse ever in any medical setting, even though she may have injured my nasal passage beyond repair.

Chapter 78

Mercury in Retrograde (Or, Everything Is Going to Shit Right Now)

I am not an astrologer. But in my experience, one does not need to be an astrologer to understand that when Mercury is in retrograde everything goes to shit. I swear, I've been feeling super burned out at work, low energy, combined with general feelings of worthlessness. And then I saw an article yesterday about Mercury being in retrograde and it all made sense. I'm pretty certain I will feel the yuckiness lifting soon, but man, I hope it hurries up.

Many times in the past I've experienced similar effects from this astrological occurrence. Or perhaps curse? I don't know. I dread this phenomenon, but I often feel a bit better when I am aware that it is in play. It gives a small amount of comfort to understand why everything sucks at certain times.

Update: Fast forward many months and...it's baaaaaaack. But I hope it won't get me as badly as last time. I am strong! I can stand up to this planetary trend that bullies unsuspecting innocent people into crumbling like small children at the drop of a hat. It's kind of funny, actually, because I wasn't even aware, yet, of disharmony this time around. A dear friend mentioned it to me. But she said it just started yesterday and is set to last almost the whole month. So...yay! Nothing I can do about it. I might as well cross my fingers, knock on some wood, and keep marching on. Besides which, it's the month of March. Damn the weird astrological phenomenons! Full steam ahead!!!

Chapter 79

Farewell, Dear Priya

While getting ready to pick up my girls from school I heard a text come in. I opened it, expecting a sweet message from Lefty, or Verizon Wireless telling me I owed some lame "overage data" charge. I was fully unprepared for what I read. The text was from Chloë telling me that Priya had died suddenly in a car accident.

DAMN IT. Beautiful Priya. The first time I met her she walked into my workplace and I was taken aback by her eyes. I felt like they were seeing into mine with a rare intensity. And her smile evoked a feeling that she knew special secrets to life she might just share with me if she were to trust me enough. Priya had come to the U.S. from India when she was ten years old. Caught between the customs of two worlds. You could sense her struggle with it. Sometimes when she came to see me she talked about a boy she liked. Sometimes she would tell me about a lost love that hurt her deeply. One time in particular, she spoke with me about her feelings surrounding arranged marriage. It seemed as if she was trying to talk herself into being okay with the inevitable. I think she assumed that would be her fate, to have a stranger picked out for her to spend the rest of her life with. I felt an indescribable sadness at the thought of her marrying in this manner. I felt protective of her, as if she were a little sister.

In saying this, I want to be clear that I mean no disrespect to Priya's wonderful family. They are amazing human beings. I just put myself in Priya's shoes and felt so sad for her to marry for custom rather than for love and passion. Because I could tell that Priya was a creature of passion and beauty, not a creature of conformity. She had a difficult time with the world because she had very high ideals for herself and others, and when things didn't go the way she wanted them to, she felt betrayed by everyone around her. I wish I could have helped her more when she came to talk to me. I listened and I cared deeply, but I wish I could have done more for her.

Priya exuded such a bright fire for life that I still find it hard to believe she's gone. I have the last texts we exchanged in my phone. Once in a while when I'm deleting old messages, I run across her last "hello" and my last "hope all is well!" When that happens I always smile for a second, then cry yet again over the realization that she's gone. I'm honored to have known such a special soul.

Chapter 80

Why Do People Not Feel More of an Obligation to Protect Women?

I was standing in my kitchen looking out the window when she came into view. She was young, wearing a mask due to the pandemic. Walking quickly like she was trying to run away from her problems. I realized that one of her problems was following her. A young man. He was yelling at her. She was trying to ignore him and keep moving forward. They stopped near the concession stand at the ballpark across from my house. I heard him call her a "dumb bitch." He was a real charmer, obviously. I almost called 911 right then and there, but for some reason I waited. That will haunt me the rest of my life.

The girl began to walk away again. I was hoping she would keep going and leave the abusive loser behind for good. But something caused her to turn around just when she was going to step out of my line of sight. She strolled slowly back to him and they slipped behind the concession building. Now I really began to worry. And at the same time I got a knock at the door. It was my sister-in-law, Heidi. She and Lefty's brother, Phousy, live next door to us, which I love.

I let her in the house and asked her if she had seen the fighting couple outside. She said yes, and then we both looked to see if they were back in sight. Low and behold, they were, and this time the motherfucker was choking the girl. Fucking Fuck!! My blood boiled and I dialed the police. He needed to go *down.* And I wanted to watch it happen from my kitchen window. I fervently hoped they would not be gentle with the creep. Maybe they would needlessly slam him to the pavement and rub his face in the granules of dislodged concrete in the parking lot? Yeah, that would be great.

The 911 operator said they would get a patrol out quickly. But, as luck would have it, they were not quick enough. Because just after my call, I saw the pair walking away from the ball park and up a side street in my neighborhood. He seemed to be dragging her along and she looked unwilling to go. She looked defeated. Like a ragdoll in the arms of a less than gentle kid who liked to toss her around too much and was bad at catching. My heart ached and I wish I had been brave enough to run outside and confront the asshole harming her. Even typing this now, months after the incident, it brings angry tears to my eyes. I want to know her name. I want to know if she is ok now.

The fucking cops finally showed up. Not one patrole car, not two, but three cars. And what did they do? Instead of spreading out and canvasing the entire neighborhood looking to save the girl, they convened in the parking lot near the ballpark for about forty-five minutes, then called me to let me know that they had looked for the couple in question but could not find them. The cop on the phone said, "Yeah, hopefully she will come to her senses and report the abuse, but I'm not gonna hold my breath." I felt sick. They obviously didn't even try to find her. Not for any reasonable period of time anyway. And then the one thing the cop could say was to insinuate that the responsibility was all on the girl to come forward? What about the fucking psycho of a guy abusing her? Was he her boyfriend? Her pimp? Who the fuck knows, but the cop had zero words regarding him. He could have said, "Yeah, I hope the guy stops being a violent douche and learns how to treat women right." But no, it was all on the girl. And the cop didn't sound like he cared one iota about her. The callousness in his voice spoke volumes. That familiar victim-blaming attitude deeply ingrained in so many institutions of American society.

To the girl I am speaking of: I am sorry I did not do enough to protect you. I am sorry our country does not value women enough to go to the ends of the earth to save them. Or at least to canvas the entire neighborhood to save *you*. I hope you survive your abuse and are able to tell your story someday. You matter. Your body matters. Your voice matters. I'm just so sorry that law enforcement and society tell you differently. And to the guy who was overpowering you: Burn in Hell, you fucking bastard.

Chapter 81

I Know Why They Don't Tell Until Ten Years Later

Lately I've been having to acknowledge that being raped years ago has been affecting me more than it used to. I wrote that first chapter about it a year and a half ago. By now it's been about nine years since the night it actually happened, and I didn't expect it to resurge like this. I didn't used to think of it and have it make me cry, but lately that's what's been happening.

Almost every day you hear in the media about a new sexual assault allegation leveled at some high-up person in power. Or at the man next door. Everyone and their brother asks, "Why didn't she go to the police when it happened? If it was that bad, why didn't she tell?"

Well, I'm here to tell you why: you don't tell the police because you feel stupid that you went home with the guy on the first date. You don't go to the police because you were drinking, too, and you feel like you shouldn't have been so foolish as to accept the drink he *brought to you.* You know you should have stuck to drinks directly handed to you by the bartender. You don't report because you really do feel like it's *your fucking fault.*

If I could go back in time I would have gone to an emergency room the next day to test for drugs in my system. I know he put something in my drink, but I will never *know* know. And that kills me.

There's this beautiful song on country radio called "Drunk Girl." It's about a man saying to take a girl home if she's drunk, let her sleep alone and lock the door on your way out. Every time it comes on I start crying. I get this lump that wells up in my throat, and my chest tightens, because my heart is beating too fast. Trying to run away from the pain. And all I can see is me back on that bed, not strong enough or possessing enough clarity of mind to push him off of me. Get him OUT of me. After an experience like this, the years don't help. They don't heal. They don't really do anything except make you more angry. More angry than you ever realized you were.

The other day I had this disturbing thought. The statute of limitations is up for my rape. I couldn't go back and legitimately do anything about it even if I wanted to now. And this got me wondering: *Who the* fuck *puts a statute of limitations on a crime that takes so much from a person?* I don't understand it. It's like they're saying there's a time limit to tell your story or else it never really happened. How convenient for all the sexual predators out there.

It happened. It sucked. And years later I'm only beginning to understand what it did to me. It's like a delayed brokenness I don't want to admit to. It makes me feel ashamed and weak. Feelings I don't like. I don't want. And I don't know how to make go away. I'm not sure if they ever will.

I think with horror about all the other millions of people who are sexually mistreated all the time, and I feel like I should be thankful I only endured it once. And it's not like I was kidnapped and tied up. I wasn't subjected to terror before it happened. I was subjected to coercion. I *should be thankful.* But it's still not okay. Nowhere near it. It started as consensual and ended as nonconsensual, painful and unprotected. And if I were able to go back in time I would have spoken some words of wisdom to myself. I would have told myself to watch out for me more. To pay better attention. To remember that not all people are safe to go home with. I would have said a lot of things, but I can't go back and do that. And I hope someday, during some type of exceptionally freeing moment, I will be able to forgive myself.

Chapter 82

Chloë's Eighteenth Birthday

I still vividly remember the day I gave birth to my four-pound, twelve-ounce adorable first born baby of mine. She was fragile and perfect. Tomorrow is her eighteenth birthday, and each time I think about it I start to cry. Not because I'm sad she's growing up to be such a wonderful person, but because I *don't understand* how time can move with such stealth. It steals things from us in broad daylight and seems to have no remorse. I've been joking for a while that I'm having an early midlife crisis, and these realizations are proof. Time simply moves too fast and I have so many items on my life goals to-do list, so it needs to chill out for a bit.

Chloë was born to my young and naive self, when I was clueless about how to be a mother, but she didn't hold it against me. She seemed to understand. We grew up together. Good pals. She opened my heart in a way I didn't know was possible. Parenting changes you. You realize that there is such a thing as boundless love. The way I love Chloë and her sister is infinite and fierce. To watch how amazing they are is sometimes strange to me. I am taken aback for a moment and have to remind myself that they once existed *inside my womb*. The miracle of life is not lost on me. I find things every day that seem like magic, not logic. For

---

Chloë reminds me of a little chipmunk here.

instance, whenever I see a rainbow, I remember biology class in high school. Learning about the spectrum of light, and why they occur. But my mind is oddly constructed and I can't break it down that way. For me, the beauty of a rainbow is caused by some magical force that likes to paint the sky on days when the sun and the rain dance together way up high. Where sadness does not exist. And the blue heavens are alight with the sound of Mozart bouncing off of every soft cloud that passes by.

I am thankful my daughters came into my life when they did. Exactly when I did not want them to. They were not part of my life plan, yet they chose me because they knew I needed them, even if I didn't know it myself at the time. They knew I would never learn the things I needed to learn without them here to teach me. They have helped me be less selfish. I'm still self centered, but *less.* They have also shown me I have a long way to go until I am commendably evolved in the way many people strive to be. When they push my buttons I tend to push back like a child myself. Rather than acting like the adult I'm supposed to be. I wonder if this is because I had them so young, or if it's how I would have been as a parent regardless what age I started the journey. But I'll never know, and that's okay with me. We've kind of raised each other, the girls and I. We are strong, stubborn, and real. We are all exactly who we were born to be. Imperfections, scars and all. And when I see Chloë and Gwen walking through this world with their heads held high, and the light of life in their beautiful eyes, I am so proud.

Chapter 83
A Bad Day

Today was a bad day. Not just a bit of an annoyance, but a really fucking *bad day*...It started out with me feeling like it was still the middle of the night when my alarm went off, and it progressed to feeling like I was falling asleep while careening down the freeway on my commute to work. Then it escalated to a point of no return when I was invited to a conference by the local transportation organization that supplies bus passes for students, and I was told by my new boss, Lisa, that I couldn't go. She indicated that somehow I wasn't "knowledgeable" enough in the area to attend as a college representative. Wow. I tried for hours not to take that personally. It didn't work. I took it personally. How else was I fucking supposed to take it? It stung so bad I had thought bubbles over my head of walking in tomorrow morning and then turning around and walking right back out, while dropping the mic and uttering, "See ya, Bitches! Especially you, Lisa."

After the comment about needing someone more knowledgeable, my boss even threw in, "And I don't remember a situation where it would be appropriate to send a part-time employee to an event like this." Excuse me? I guess I was unaware until that moment that part-time employees were considered inferior to other workers at my college. Definitely did not get the memo. You know how there are moments when a lightbulb goes on above your head and you are suddenly aware that people were looking down at you the entire time, but you were too busy trying to survive your miserable job to see it? Well, this was that moment for me. It was crushing and embarrassing.

I know Mercury is in retrograde (yes, again), and my Aries horoscope pointed to discontent at work today (which I didn't realize until recounting my bad day to my daughter, Gwen, and she pulled it up and showed me), but I can't help but feel like this weird day is yet another aspect of the universe telling me I'm in the wrong place at the wrong time. Wrong, wrong, wrong. All wrong.

The strangest part is that my new boss is a wonderful person. Truly. I honestly mean that. A quite amazing woman. A woman who appears to be compassionate right down to her very soul. So the last thing I expected from her was to feel so demeaned. It is disconcerting to encounter painful friction in completely unexpected places. And I want to note that I know she didn't try to make me feel that way on purpose, but...*damn*. It really knocked me down at a time when I was already pretty much immobilized on the floor. To sink lower, I'd have to crawl underneath the office and hang out with the rattlesnakes. (The campus has an infestation of them. I'm not joking. Sometimes the security guards find as many as six rattlesnakes in one day on campus grounds).

But I don't know, perhaps it is a gift from the universe that this whole mess came up, because it's making me reevaluate my life. Sometimes the unexpectedly yucky times spur us towards positive change. And then at some point we can look back and thank the figures who brought up such bad feelings and realizations deep within us.

Please let me look back someday and understand that this was really what today was all about. Giving me a demeaning but firm nudge in the right direction. Kicking me in the backside and saying, "Girl, get yourself out of here! You're crazy to be killing time in an environment that doesn't see your value, and the sand in your hourglass is running out fast. Save yourself while you have the strength to do so."

It's late and I'm going to make myself get some sleep now. Actually, that's a lie. What I'm really going to do is go get ready for bed, lay down and loop negative thoughts about what transpired earlier today. And I'm going to do that over and over and over again. But I'm hoping to get at least a little rest so I can go back to my wrong job tomorrow and get serious about brainstorming more ways to live my life right. There's a voice in my head screaming at me, "Now is the time. *NOW IS THE TIME, ARIANNA!*"

Chapter 84

Stuff

Gwen and I recently spent the day helping my mom clean out her cabin. The one I was born in. She's trying to get a handle on her paperwork and extra things she doesn't need. In the process we came across so many memories. Ghosts hung out with us while we shuffled and sorted. Lamented and laughed. We found old letters from my sister. One from when she was eighteen and working for Greenpeace in Amherst, Massachusetts. She was complaining about the fact that no one took her seriously because she was so young and had what a guy called, "Cute, pinchable cheeks." That really got her goat. I was not surprised. Calling Naomi cute would definitely have been fighting words to her. She was a five-foot, two-inch ball of feminist fire. This guy probably regretted messing with her. I'm sure she sufficiently took him down a notch in his masculinity. She was practically a professional at lowering the male ego.

We also found old poems from my grandpa Herman. One that described Mom, me, and my girls as "Angelic Beings." This made me emotional. I've been so upset with him, even after his passing, for not being more caring towards my mom, but his sweet poem felt like he was saying hello from beyond the grave. Like he was telling all of us that he really did love us. It felt important in the healing process of icky family drama. Then the real kicker, which left no eye dry in the house, was when Gwen came across another poem. This one an apology from Herman to his dead son, Konstantine, Mom's older brother who died of AIDS when I was very young. He was a gay activist and journalist in San Francisco. There's a clip of him in the film "Milk" in the Mission District with a smile that spans miles. Reading a verdict he was happy about in the day's newspaper. Herman's poem apologized to his son for not understanding him. Not being there for him when he was needed. It was a reminder that my grandpa was capable of deeper emotions and compassion. Something I didn't usually see him exhibit towards anyone but himself.

I came across old photos from the memorial in Hawaii for my sister. The one I couldn't attend, though I did participate in the gathering we had later in California. The pictures kind of ripped off some old scabs on my heart I thought had fallen off a long time ago. It just never ends. Grief *never ends.* And that's okay.

I told my mom I could really understand why she didn't want to sort through all this stuff alone. Because it wasn't just stuff. It was *stuff. INTENSE* STUFF. She said thank you to me in a way that made me realize she's been needing someone to understand that for a long time. Just needing support in cleaning up forty years of memories that she shouldn't have to face on her own. Memories of beauty and pain. And most are a mix of both. My mom is incredible. I'm so proud to be her daughter.

In that old log cabin, with three generations of women working together, I felt centuries of female lineage, female power coursing through our veins. Struggles and triumphs. Voices screaming out to be heard. And taken seriously. If there's one thing that women really want, it's to be taken seriously when we speak. We are not simply accessories for a man's arm, but full, strong beings. We still turn on the TV and see half-naked cheerleaders in the NFL who get paid minimum wage. We see bikini-clad girls parade themselves around at high-profile wrestling and MMA fighting matches. They aren't given names or roles in tune with who they are, they are there for decoration. They are there so guys can drool over them and say to their buddies, "That's a nice piece of ass."

And on this topic, I'm always trying to figure out, if I ever get into incredible shape again, would I do something like this, if asked? Would I want to be displayed solely for my body and my beauty and nothing else? I hope not, because all it does is send demeaning messages to young girls watching the screen and taking it all in without a filter. Beauty is great. There's nothing wrong with beauty. The trouble starts when that's all a woman is expected to be. Because youth fades, and wrinkles form. And women need to have a more multifaceted game plan for a fulfilling life.

It meant so much to me to have Gwen help us during our cabin work. She is such a strong girl. Already, she's had too many disturbing interactions with teenage boys who don't know what respecting girls means. They don't know what it looks like. They've never been taught, or they don't care to learn. She walks through her own anxiety-prone storm every day at her high school and yet retains who she is. And who she is is nothing short of incredible. She teaches me so much in her example and I am extremely thankful.

Chapter 85

Loneliness

I'm three days in with eating less. Enough. I'm not starving myself. But eating *less.* Maybe twelve to fifteen hundred calories per day. I guess instead of less I could say "the right amount." I've been experiencing an extreme feeling of loneliness, and I'm starting to think this is what I've been running from my whole life. Not loneliness as in I want someone other than my husband, loneliness as in I want him to hold me tightly and never, ever, ever let go. It's like I need to just melt into him and have him protect me from the world and myself.

I've been thinking a lot about times in my past when I've put on weight. One of the first times I can pinpoint was when I found out my ex-husband cheated on me. I was so shocked and hurt. And it immediately gave me that sense that I "wasn't enough." I'm pretty sure I unconsciously said to myself, "I am young and beautiful, and in darn good shape yet he found the need to sleep with someone who wasn't me." I couldn't come to any other conclusion than the fact that the girl he cheated with must have been skinnier. He told me that wasn't the case, but his words didn't take any of the sting away. I'm not certain I've ever felt "enough" again. Sometimes we think those old hurts have healed, only to find that there's a whole storage closet full of more hurt. We closed the door and forgot about it long, long ago, but just because you forget about something doesn't mean it disappears. It's still there and I'm really not in the mood to sort through it right now.

This is where I would normally go get a snack. Have some ice cream, (I'm out at the moment), or perhaps a piece of sourdough toast and butter. But I'm gonna try experiencing, like *really experiencing* my buried pain tonight. I will snack on unexplored disappointment with a side of extreme fear regarding when and how it might ever go away.

My theory heads more and more towards traumatic experiences being the cause of my weight issues. I think I eat so I don't feel. I'm pretty sure I also started gaining weight after I was unfaithful to David. And after being raped. There are various times I can pinpoint where I started covering myself up with food. And I didn't even see that I was doing it at the time.

Another side effect of three days of eating carefully and not trashing my system is feeling a certain type of power resurging through my veins. A strength I only seem to utilize when I'm going through a tough break-up or have suffered some other kind of deep disappointment. It's got me wondering, *Why do I normally suppress this inner power by overeating?* I mean, why would I do that to myself? Is it just because I get overly hungry with hormone fluctuations and then can't get back on track? It doesn't make sense to me.

So counterintuitive not to want this inborn power at my fingertips at all times. It's a weird combination. Powerful loneliness. Lonely power. I'm going to sit with it tonight. It's not going to feel good. That's okay. Let's see what tomorrow brings.

Chapter 86

Snow!

I couldn't believe my eyes. White stuff was falling from the sky like I hadn't seen in so long. I moved from the mountains of Trinity County to Redding about three years ago. Since then I've had to train myself to stop hoping for snow each winter. It doesn't snow in Redding. But last night and this morning was another story! About eight inches fell overnight and I am overwhelmed with the feeling of nostalgia and magic. It's practically a miracle!

Part of me is thinking, *This must be due to global warming. Such odd weather patterns.* But for just this moment I'm going to allow myself to be swept away by the mystery of it all, and not feel worried or guilty about the origin of this unexpected storm.

My husband woke me up as he was getting ready for work. Around 5:00 a.m. He said, "I think the power's out. And there's tons of snow out

---

A snowy trail I used to love in Trinity County.

there." He called in to his boss and she said don't bother coming in. Plus our kids' school is canceled, which I thought would be very exciting for them. Turns out it's exciting for Chloë and Cameron, but not so much for Gwen, who cried because she still misses Trinity County, and the snow makes her miss it more. I felt badly that I was so surprised by her reaction. Here I am excited as Hell about something that isn't even supposed to happen here, and all it did was bring on the blues for my girl. She said mostly it's because she hasn't been awakened and told it's a snow day since she lived part-time with her dad. I think she misses her father. Seeing her sad makes me sad, too.

Life is unpredictable. Something that makes someone want to go dance in the street with happiness can make someone else crumble under the sadness of old memories. There's no one way for people to react, and that can be both wonderful and tragic at the same time.

Last night when the snow started to come down, I was so in awe that I snapped a few short videos of it in the glow of the street lights. It was absolutely mesmerizing. The second clip I took had the faint sound of a train horn in the background. Passing through my town from an unknown origin, and moving on to who-knows-where. Trains and snow are two things that induce instant wonder for me. They evoke a similar feeling of mystery and intrigue. Snow because it's so damn beautiful and elusive around my neck of the woods, and trains because they symbolize what has been, and what is yet to be. I've always loved to look at trains and wonder where they're going, what's their story?

There is a train that ventures past my campus at work every day. Sometimes coming, sometimes going. I can see it out the window from my desk. It stirs an emotion in me every single time. Makes me want to hop on and ask it to take me away. Away from my office phone ringing off the hook while I'm trying to assist ten too many people. It's such a strong feeling that comes up inside me each time that I recently wrote a song simply called "Train." I hope to get the chance to record it and, perhaps, put it on my next album. It's a little bit of a downer, but so is life. I think people can handle it.

For the moment I guess I may go back to sleep. My head soft on the pillow like the blanket of white encapsulating us right now. I feel lucky in this dark house with candles lit. The power may be out for the long haul today. An unusual occurrence, because, like I said, "It doesn't snow in Redding."

Chapter 87

Alpha Female

Mr. Blues Man is a walking legend. His voice is every bit as good as Ray Charles or Otis Redding. Years ago he met my brother and our friend, Jim Hyatt, in Nashville while opening for *his* friend Etta James. Yes...Etta freakin' James. Now he lives in a spot out in the middle of nowhere, here in California.

I've spent countless hours recording with Mr. Blues Man at his home and enduring his quirky producer ways. He can go from funny and easy-going to hyper-sensitive, controlling, and downright intimidating in a matter of seconds. But I still believe in his musical genius, even though I refuse to work with him anymore. He's so full of soul that he taught me a lot over the years. He inspired me. He still inspires me.

Mr. Blues Man asked me to come out and record with him several years ago. Since it meant driving out to a remote area to meet someone I didn't know yet, I made the natural choice and asked my mom to come along with me. And my oh my, he flirted with her shamelessly the first time he met her. And the second time. And the third...

He's a seasoned blues singer and prolific songwriter. A music business guy down to the bone. He walks and talks melodies, bridges, and hooks. He also has a pretty intense narcissistic personality coupled with an overly inflated ego. I've created so much music with him that has never seen the light of day. I listen to old tracks on my phone or computer sometimes and get the chills, because a lot of it is *good.* I'm proud of it. But everytime he and I thought we were on course to complete a project together, something would happen to stall it or run it off the tracks. I tried until recently to song-write with him, but then he made the mistake of saying something stupid to me. Before I tell you what that stupid thing was, I should tell you that Mr. Blues Man is a control freak. And he has to be the alpha in the room. Always the man with the plan. When he senses that someone around him is getting too comfortable, he does something to throw them off-guard and make them demure and unsure of themselves. So, one day I was singing some of my recent songs for him. I wanted him to put instrumentation to them. See, I write with lyrics and melodies, but no instruments. I've been told a million times I should play this or I should play that. I did play fiddle and piano as a kid. But instruments are not where it's at for me. I found that out a long time ago. My passion is in my voice, my words, and how they can connect with the deepest emotions of an audience.

Like I said, I was singing some of my newer songs for him when he stopped me and said, "Ari, you've gotta stop saying that you've 'written these songs.' You haven't written them. You have *song ideas*. That's all."

I could feel my cheeks get red hot with anger. And then of course my eyes welled up with tears. But I tried hard to keep my voice from shaking when I let him have it. I shot him down like a bird out of the sky and told him to never talk to me like that again. I told him that the lyrics and melody *are what songs are made of.* And that, just because I write a cappella does not mean I am any less of a songwriter than anyone else.

Let me tell you a secret: When I gave him all this attitude back in his face I was practically dissolving with self doubt. Self doubt induced by his demeaning words. But I felt this intense need to fight back and stare him down. I was so tired of being told stupid shit from men in the music industry. Shit meant to tear me down instead of build me up. Exhausted with not being taken seriously as a female singer/songwriter. As a whole individual who has a lot to offer to the world of music. Besides which, when I write a song I believe in, the next thing I do is find a musician to put instrumentation to it. The people I work with are called co-writers. Ever heard of 'em? It just doesn't seem that unusual to me.

After that day I exchanged a few more emails with him about some co-writes, but I just couldn't shake what he had said to me. I felt like he tackled me from behind and tried to steal my dreams. And I couldn't forgive him for it. It wasn't long before he took a very controlling tone with me again, via email, and that was the point when I told him that I admired his talent, I believed in his music (still do), but I refused to deal with his abusive, control freak behavior anymore. I was done. Out. Gone.

"Gone" is actually the name of one of my songs we collaborated on. I still haven't decided whether I'll release it someday with the parts he contributed to, in which case I'll credit him as a co-writer, or if I will just revert back to my original version and go it alone. But it feels good to know it's my decision, and he can't take that away from me.

I wish Mr. Blues Man well. I love his music. And I love him like family, but our falling out may last for the long haul, because I don't plan on backing down anytime soon. At this point in my life and career there's only room for one alpha in the room, and she's me.

Chapter 88

Aren't We All Kind of like Spies?

Lefty and I have recently been hooked on "The Americans." It's an intricate television series about Russian spies living in the U.S. Raising their two kids. Trying to blend in and be good parents one moment and switching into cold-blooded killer mode the next. Some of their victims deserve their fates. Others were just in the wrong place at the wrong time.

This show has me thinking about how it's just an exaggeration of real life. No, not the murder part. I don't condone violence. But about wearing five different hats every day and trying to juggle our inner and outer personas while staying true to ourselves. Throughout a lifetime, doesn't it seem like we have many different lives wrapped into one? I'm not the same person I was when I was locked into my first marriage. And you are probably not the same person you were many years ago either. We change with the seasons. The years give us beautiful gifts, and the years take away our youth. The things we loved and the things we hated about it.

We survive this odd venture by constantly adapting to outside influences, and sometimes wearing disguises like spies on TV. We laugh when we want to cry. Because maybe we are not around people we feel safe with yet. We pretend something doesn't hurt because we know the person who said hurtful words to us *wants to watch us hurt.* And we don't want to give them that satisfaction.

Maybe in some weird way, we are all just spies faking our way through our daily breaths. Faking it 'til we can be at the place where we are truly making it. I don't know, but I do find it fascinating how much we learn and grow each year. Each decade. Each quarter of a century. We are expansive beings who do not need to stay confined to only one identity each time we're born. And as far as I'm concerned, as long as we're not murdering anyone, we might as well try on as many hats as we want, if it makes us happy. Today, I think I'll choose the one with sequins and a peacock feather tucked into the brim. Lively, vibrant, a bit mysterious. I am all those things and more...and so are you.

Chapter 89

Helicopter Parent: Guilty as Charged

I'm that mom who calls you five times in a row if you don't pick up your phone when you're away from home. If you're my kid, you'd better get used to me demanding accountability about where you are and who you are with at all times. I'm kind of like a drill sergeant in that way. I try hard to realize that someday I'm gonna need to let my kids be a bit more independent, but that day is not today, or tomorrow, or next year.

My need to keep close track of my children stems from loving them so fiercely. It stems from the fact that I would never forgive myself if something bad happened to them that I could have prevented. This need probably also stems from the fact that I am a control freak with some type of undiagnosed anxiety disorder and I worry nonstop if I can't reach my kids within five minutes of contacting them. I'm a little afraid of how much I've damaged them with my behavior. I would imagine it induces a lot of anxiety when they know their mother is going to completely freak out the second she can't reach them.

I realize that me keeping close tabs on my children is a reaction to growing up with too much freedom. I'm glad I survived, but my friends were a whole lot wilder than I was and I put myself in some not-so-safe situations. This was before the age of cell phones and I don't know how my parents didn't lose their minds. Luckily I wasn't a kid who thought I was invincible, so I did try to be careful, but I was still young and stupid plenty of the time.

When my girls were toddlers, my mom took them to the coast for a fun trip to the beach. I expected to hear from them when they got there so I knew they had arrived in one piece. As the evening wore on, no calls came. It turned into the middle of the night, the phone did not ring. This was still before my mom or I ever had a cell phone, so I was reliant on her to get in touch with me. I couldn't call her because there was no place to call. I became rigid with fear that my little girls and my mom had catapulted off a cliff and were lifeless at the bottom of a river. Panic is not a strong enough word to describe how I felt. I was paralyzed with tension and worry that I would never hold my kids in my arms again.

All of this and, of course, I was home alone, while my ex-husband was off who-knows-where. This goes down in my memory as one of the worst nights of my life (obviously you know from reading this book that there've been several). I heard from my mom the next morning, and she thought I was at her house for the night instead of mine, so she left a voicemail on her cabin phone for me. Utter panic on my part, fun on the coast for them. Thank God they were alright. And thank God for the rise of cellular technology today. It's both a blessing and a curse, but when I'm trying to track down my children, it's the most wonderful thing in the world.

Chapter 90

Cross-Country Chaos

Years ago my mom and I decided to drive across the country to visit my brother in Nashville. We figured we would see the sights along the way and it would be a grand adventure. Well, we saw a lot of sights, but it was mostly a nightmare. The driving was so time-consuming that when we got there I was already having a panic attack about driving back. It took us four solid days in the car. We did choose to stop at hotel rooms each night instead of driving straight through. My least favorite spot was a seedy motel in Colorado. I have never felt more certain I was going to be murdered in the middle of the night. Terrifying! The front door didn't even lock right and I swear I slept with one eye open.

For some reason there was something that disturbed me about Colorado in general. It was stunning to look at. All the beautiful rock formations and train tunnels, but there was something about it I can only describe as bad energy. I wondered if there was some type of magnetism in the rocks that didn't agree with the energy field of my being. Sorry if you're reading this and you're from Colorado. I'm sure you have found the good aspects I could not.

I loved seeing all the amazing table-top mountains along the way. Some looked so ancient I half expected to look up and see dinosaurs roaming the ridge tops. They took my breath away, even amidst the delirium of too much driving. We never did venture out to see the Grand Canyon, which I regret now. I have never seen it in person. But the little bit of extra traveling to that famed location seemed altogether insane. I couldn't do it.

I don't remember much from the actual time we spent in Nashville once we got there. But I know we had a good visit with my brother and his friends. The one night that sticks out in my mind I do vividly recall was under a mesmerizing full moon when we all jumped in the lake where our friend's houseboat was docked. We were having a blissful time swimming and drinking, until someone mentioned large fish with teeth, water moccasins, and snapping turtles. That was it. I was done. I couldn't get out of the water fast enough.

Mom and I spent four days driving to Tennessee, four days there, and four days driving back. Not an efficient use of travel time, but I'm glad we did it once. Never again. At least not without having about a month to stop and stay at fun places along the way.

Chapter 91

Chinese Astrology

Fun fact: I was born in the year of the rooster. Which most people call the year of the cock. Yes. There are tigers, dragons, horses, and other very cool creatures. I had to be born in the year of the cock. I'm reminded of this sore spot in my ego every time I'm at a Chinese restaurant. I look down with envy at some of the other animals on my paper place setting. I guess I could also have been a rat like my parents. But even that is a little less embarrassing than being a…*cock*.

And in case you haven't already noticed, I have about a seventh-grade maturity level when it comes to my sense of humor. So, whenever this topic comes up among friends and whatnot, I cannot simply state what sign I was born under. No, I start giggling like a school girl about my silly misfortune as I explain it, and inevitably end up just drawing more attention to the subject than I wanted to in the first place.

On the bright side, my husband Lefty is the year of the snake. And that makes us the perfect match. So, for him I will endure my embarrassment the rest of my life. And I'll endure it with a smile on my face.

Chapter 92

Sewing Needles

Gwen has an adorably dangerous habit of forgetting where she put the sewing needle every fucking time she finishes a sewing project. I'll exclaim in shock over and over again that she *has got to be more cautious* and only place them in the little sewing-kit-cushion-thingy or on her dresser, desk, or some other hard surface away from bare feet or unsuspecting fleshy butts. But despite my dramatic lectures and exasperated looks, I inevitably find needles on a regular basis, stuck halfway into a couch cushion or on her bedroom carpet.

The weirdest example of this bizarrely nonchalant, caution-be-damned approach of Gwen's was when I made a large batch of brown rice one evening. We usually buy it from the bulk bins at our favorite grocery store, so it's just stored in a thin plastic bag. Miss Gwendolyn must have made a project involving not only sewing, but also dried brown rice. I was scooping most of it into a tupperware container to place in the fridge before bedtime and to my abject horror I spotted a piece of pink thread cooked into the kernels of rice as I transferred it. And what might you guess was connected to the thread at the end? Yes. A large, oddly evil looking silver sewing needle that, by the grace of God, had not ended up in the generous helping of vegetable stir fry and rice I ate earlier that very night for dinner.

Yep, I definitely dodged a bullet there and the next morning had an interesting conversation *yet again* with Gwen about her need to recognize that needles are dangerously sharp, harmful objects that require treating with a type of caution she was apparently not born with, and may in fact never be able to cultivate during her lifespan here on earth.

Chapter 93

Tattoos

In a couple of days I'm going with Chloë to get her first tattoo. Not my idea, this is all her, but she is eighteen now and I am aware I can guide her choices at this point but I can't control them. Though I do still keep extreme tabs on her, as I mentioned a few pages ago. I would try to put my foot down if she planned tattooing something really stupid on her body. Like a skull with blood coming out of its eyes, or a saying that included the F word. But she's not getting something stupid, she's getting something really quite thoughtful. Something I don't think she will regret. It's a pretty design of the seven chakras on the inner side of her wrist. Very small and delicate. Just like her.

I don't know why I was so shocked a long time ago when she started talking about tattoos she wanted. I should have known to expect this. Her dad is covered in tattoos and I have six myself. Also her stepfather has beautiful tattoos all up and down his arms. I love his.

Love.

Mine started with a butterfly in the middle of my chest, on my sternum. Basically between my breasts so, needless to say, it's not noticeable to the public most of the time. I got it when I was about twenty. It's in honor of my sister. Before she died she told a friend she would be a butterfly. To this day, I never see a butterfly without thinking of her.

My second tattoo was the cardinal sin of all tattoos. The real taboo kind. No, not a phallic symbol on my leg, but my ex-husband's name. I got that, of course, when we were still married. The third was a small apple blossom on my foot. My gift to myself for my thirtieth birthday during a trip to Nashville. The next one is the word LOVE on the inside of my left forearm. That came after the particularly traumatic break-up with David. It was my way of reminding myself what is really important. I wanted it in a place I would see every day. It was my way of saying to him, “David, you will not steal my ability to love!” I knew I was at risk of being bitter from all the heartache, and I just couldn’t let myself become that kind of person.

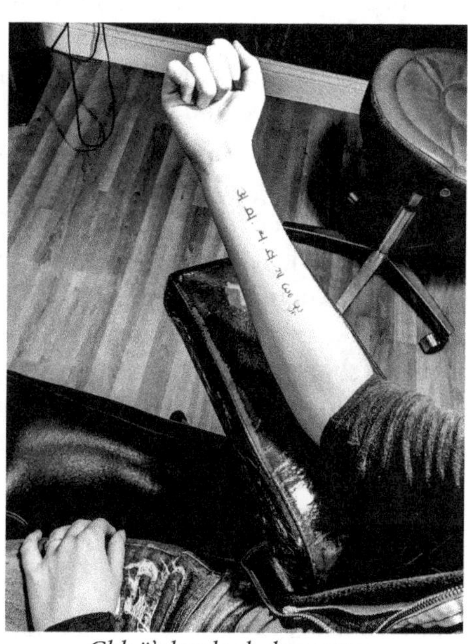

Chloë’s lovely chakra tattoo.

My fifth tattoo is covering my second one. Yep, got that ex’s name inked over with a couple black roses. It’s actually my favorite tattoo. The guy did a great job. The name underneath is just a silent memory now, and I think Lefty probably appreciates that, too.

Last, I have three large roses starting at my right shoulder and flowing down almost to my elbow. I like them, but I don’t think they are finished. I need something more, but I’m not going to get that something until the vision becomes crystal-clear.

So, back to Miss Chloë: How could I be surprised when she wanted to follow in all her parents’ footsteps and get artwork permanently etched on her body? I don’t know. It’s just a glaring reminder that she is really growing up. But I’m so proud of the woman she has become. So sweet and so bold. The heart of an activist. The soul of an artist. I will try to be strong while I hold her hand in that tattoo parlor. I still don’t understand where her childhood has gone.

Chloë’s lovely chakra tattoo.

Chapter 94

Vince

I don't remember who introduced me to him. His voice was gravelly like that actor on "Chicago P.D." Short, bald, muscular. His name was Vince and he became one of my favorite music pals. He loved to have me record vocals for some of the songs he wrote. We spent countless hours in his home studio. Take after take. Laugh after laugh. The way I'm describing it may sound like the beginning of a love story, but that was not the case. I did love him dearly, but not in a romantic way. In the way that his friendship meant so much to me and he helped inspire my creativity.

I think Vince felt safe hanging out with me. Though he was a very private person, he would sometimes share some of the past details of his life. He was haunted by experiences he had as a young man fighting for the Israeli army. And although he was quite the rebel at heart, I believe he had a short stint in law enforcement down in Southern California. But mostly, Vince was a mysterious guy whom I didn't push to share with me anything more than he wanted to. Our bond was music. And when it came to that, we were thick as thieves.

One day I got a call from him. He told me he had been diagnosed with cancer. I froze. I was so worried. Vince smoked like a chimney, and I guess it caught up with him. Or at least that was the quickest way to draw a correlation as to the cause of his ailment. He received aggressive chemo for a time. It was touch-and-go as to whether it was helping at first. But then one day, out of the blue, he showed up at the elementary school where I worked. He was there to pick up his daughter and he looked like he had a new lease on life. He gave me a big hug and said he had beaten it. The cancer was gone. Out of all the music we created together, hearing his words made the most beautiful melody of all.

But his upturn didn't last. A few months later I got a call from his girlfriend. She was letting me know his cancer had returned. This time in his brain. I never saw him again.

Friends of his held a memorial at the edge of the river by their house. It was exactly the kind of gathering Vince would have wanted. I can still hear his voice the way he answered the phone when I called to say hello.

He would always pick up and say, "Arianna, how are you…" More a statement than a question. His deep voice full of caring. I miss that voice, that man, that friendship. I'm sad for all the songs we didn't get to write together. I still feel his presence sometimes. I know he's looking down on me, wondering when I'm going to get my act together and actually release my all-original album.

As soon as I finish this book, that's the next project on my list, Vince. And it will include "Number for Heaven," a song I wrote for you. It will be soon, Vince, I promise. It will be soon.

Chapter 95

The Yes Committee

Like I told you at the beginning of this book, I never went to Kindergarten or first grade. Much less preschool. So the first time I tried attending public school in second grade was a difficult experience. I was a weird kid. I was raised doing pretty much whatever I wanted, within reason, and it was very difficult to adjust to being around a bunch of rowdy kids who were strangers. I hated how loud the cafeteria was. It gave me a stomach ache just setting foot in that big, intimidating building.

Homeschooling had given me a uniqueness that wasn't embraced by the other kids. But that was okay. I didn't want to embrace them, either. Mostly I hung around my beloved teacher and also the very kind teacher's aide who worked in her classroom.

This was so long ago that I can't remember how many of my sick days I faked versus how many I legitimately felt too sick to go to class. The school started bugging my parents because I was absent too often. What they really bugged them about is that they were losing money on the days I wasn't there. Why can't schools just tell it like it is, instead of pretending they care about the student? They just want their paycheck for each day the kids are there. Believe me, there are many great teachers and school employees, but schools as a whole have become all about the bottom line. Individual children matter less and less each year.

The school made my mom attend some meetings at a "Yes" committee to try to make her force me to go to school more often. I, in turn, began to feel sicker and sicker. Starting with debilitating stomach aches which actually continued through my childhood and into my late teens. I suppose it was connected to my anxiety issues, but I didn't know this at the time, nor did my parents. I just remember this feeling of terror and despair every time I had to be in my classroom. I felt completely panicked and trapped. Welcome to the real world, kid, right? But I didn't simply need an adjustment period, I needed to get out of there, and get out fast.

After six months at elementary school, my parents pulled me out and put me back into the homeschooling program. Six miserable months that scarred me enough that I didn't try the public school option again until the sixth grade. At that point I commuted with my dad to the school where he taught music, in the neighboring town an hour away. Luckily this second go-around went pretty well. I was such a dork, but even the popular kids took me under their wings and befriended me. I was very fortunate that a lot of them liked my dad as a teacher, and I think that fondness trickled down to me. And I guess it didn't hurt that I was rather pretty as well. They were surprisingly accepting of this new kid not well versed in popular culture or grade-level math.

I have fond memories from my years at that elementary school. Not all the memories are good, but most are, and that's nice to be able to say. I went through eighth grade and graduated. Then chose to continue on with my friends in high school. Homeschooling allowed me to find out who I was without other kids telling me who I was or labeling me with stickers I didn't like. I credit my parents and the homeschooling they did with me in creating an independent thinker. Not a crowd-follower. Crowd-following is only okay if you are immersed in an exceptionally conscious crowd, but let's face it, that's not usually the case in our odd society. My unique nature sometimes causes problems for me, but mostly it has saved me in many wonderful ways over the years. I'm content with who I am and how I became this way.

Chapter 96

My Husband Has the BEST Sense of Humor

Lefty makes me laugh. Every day. His joy is contagious and his sense of humor is witty and boyish. Charming. So damn charming. We were at our favorite restaurant tonight, called Thai Hut, when he pulled out one of his favorite jokes: He ordered a Thai beer, started drinking it, and said to me, "See Honey? I like my beer just like you like your husband: Imported." 555! He kills me. And I can't remember if I've already mentioned this, but instead of the abbreviation "Lol" we use "555." Because the number five sounds like "Ha" in Lao, 555 translates to, "HaHaHa!"

Everyone who knows Lefty knows he's really into his hair. As he should be. He's definitely got great hair. I've never seen him without his beloved blonde highlights. And when he gets a haircut that fade better be on point, or else he will not, I repeat: will *not* be a repeat customer. He jokingly wonders how many people have lost their lives due to giving Kim Jong Un a bad fade. Goodness. Scary thought.

My husband is a routine jokester, but when I need him to be serious or momentarily selfless, he's right there for me. With compassion, concern, and understanding. I know how lucky we are to have each other. And for the record: I would love him whether or not he was "imported." 555.

Chapter 97

Sneaking Out at Night (Or, I Love You, Gwen, but Don't Give Your Mother a Heart Attack!)

I woke up groggy as hell on a Saturday morning Lefty didn't have to work. An unusual occurrence. He'd been awake for hours by the time I stumbled out into the living room and gave him a good morning kiss. Comfy on the couch, he was relaxing and watching a movie. I sat down and started watching with him. When I did, I noticed he seemed stressed, but I didn't put too much thought into it. Figuring he was just sleepy and ready for a morning nap. But a few minutes later he looked at me and asked, "Did Gwen go somewhere last night? I mean, she's here now, but I couldn't sleep in the middle of the night, came out to the couch around 3:00 a.m., and ten minutes later, she came walking through the kitchen door" (coming from the garage).

A shocked expression crept across my face. I said, "Oh my God."

At that point I knew she must have hopped the fence in the backyard and gone somewhere. Like the pitbull mixes we used to have. Don't get me wrong, I'm not trying to put my child down by comparing her to a dog. I loved those dogs, and I love her. But out of all the behavior issues I've had to deal with since giving birth to my kids, I think this broke my mama heart the most. And it scared me to death.

Gwen was still asleep in her bed, so I texted her and said I knew she had come in through the garage at 3:00 a.m., and that she'd better be ready to explain where she was and what she was doing. I told her to think long and hard before she answered me, because I was not going to tolerate her messing around and giving me some made-up story. This behavior crossed a serious line, and it was making me re-evaluate my entire parenting career. I asked her point blank: "What did I do wrong in raising you?"

A while later she texted back and said she was sorry, and that she had snuck out to hang out with a couple of her friends who live in the neighborhood. I was relieved she didn't deny she had gone out, but I also didn't believe she had been visiting her girlfriends. I was pretty positive she was hanging out with a boy who lived close by. A boy she used to date and seemed to be talking to again. He was her boyfriend a couple years ago and it didn't go so well for a reason I won't go into here.

When I went into her room to talk, I of course broke down crying. This was just all too much. I said to her with anger in my eyes, "You could have been killed out there! What the hell do I need to do with you? And what do you think would have happened if I had woken up in the middle of the night to find that you were not in your bed??! You know me well enough to know that I would have *LOST MY MIND WITH WORRY.* And you're ok with taking that risk? With doing that to me??"

At this point my emotions became too much for me. I said, with my voice shaking, "I love you, and you are being more selfish and self-centered than I could have ever imagined. And your risk-taking is extremely concerning." Then I took Gwen's phone and myself out of her room.

I had to cry it out for a while. There was this terrible feeling I was completely losing my daughter. Her actions, though some would say were just typical stupid teenage antics, hit me like a ton of bricks. And I couldn't help but compare them a bit to things her father used to do. Making it all about him. Not caring how he was affecting the people around him. I realized I've always been worried about either of my girls going down a path similar to their dad's. Addiction and frequent dishonesty like it's no big deal. I don't want that to be who Gwen grows up to become. Her father is certainly not all bad. I give him a lot of credit that the girls know how much he loves them. Their bond is still there because he cultivated a strong connection with them while they were little. But there's always been too much questionable behavior and vigilante attitude built into his personality.

I don't really know how I'm going to sleep tonight. I still have Gwen's phone, and I'm going to take her computer, iPod, and her sister's older phone out of her room before bedtime so she can't get the bright idea to communicate with her on-again off-again boyfriend and run away again. But what if that doesn't stop her? You can't exactly put teenagers on a runner so they stay in one place like a puppy. And really, that's not even nice to do to a puppy, but sometimes it's the only way to keep it safe from dangers beyond the fence. I don't have plans to set up an extensive set of security cameras at the house, though this makes me seriously contemplate the possibility. What I want is for Gwen to care enough about rules and boundaries so that she won't do this again. But this is actually the third time she's shocked me with her choices. The third and most serious. And I'm at a loss. Feeling like I wouldn't mind passing the parenting on to a grandparent for a week or two. I didn't sign up for this.

My mind keeps reminding me that some of her rebellious nature comes from me, too. It has to. I'd be crazy to deny it. But when I was a kid, if I had snuck out, there wouldn't be anywhere to go. Maybe walk to a cow pasture? Or stop in to say hello to the elderly neighbors a mile down the dirt road? Obviously that wasn't a pastime at my house. Though my parents did give me a lot more freedom than I give my children. With Chloë, I'm getting used to the fact that she's almost moved out. She's a young adult now. So weird to say, but true. And when she got together with her boyfriend about a year ago, I helped her with birth control choices. Believe me, it was the last thing I wanted to be dealing with at the time. But I knew if I didn't help her deal with the situation early on, she was likely to end up a much-too-young mother like I was. I couldn't bare that thought. I want Chloë and Gwen to live their lives as full adults before they decide if they want to have kids of their own. I want them to experience what it's like to become a well rounded person before they become a parent. And then maybe they can tell me what it's like, because I have no clue.

Gwen and Chloë are both very smart girls. I raised them to talk to me as much as possible when they have a problem. I tried so hard to keep our lines of communication open, so we can stay close and I can still have a hand in keeping them safe and guiding their life choices. And I debated long and hard about even including this chapter in my book, because I don't want to give the impression that I am trying to publicly shame Gwen over what happened. Public shaming is never a good answer. But I believe public sharing sometimes can be. Maybe you're reading this and have the same issues coming up with your own children, or maybe it will take you back to your teen years, and you'll remember to have a bit more compassion for what you put your parents through.

Regardless, as a mother, I'm at a crossroads I've never been to before. I don't know what to do, and none of my options seem good. There are only bad and worse ideas about deterring this "sneaking out" behavior from happening again. And I'm contemplating making a counseling appointment for Gwen and me to attend together. Luckily, she, Chloë and I all attend therapy sessions once in a while as individuals. I'm a big believer in the power of self care and using therapy as a tool for deeper understanding of our thought patterns and behavior tendencies. I just don't know. Will it help in this situation?

I told Gwen I'm always willing to talk to her if she feels like my rules are squishing her independence. It may not change my mind about the way I parent, but I will try harder to listen, under the condition that she never, EVER, chooses the low road and leaves without my permission again. That is not an acceptable option on our table. And I also told her that if she does make that ridiculous decision again, I will have no problem pulling her out of school and putting her on independent study for a good long while. I'll let her get REALLY sick of being home with me, then see if she wants to behave better so she can go back to school.

Good Lord, I need strength.

Chapter 98

Kitten with a Red Collar

I looked out my kitchen window and saw the cutest little gray and black striped kitty with a bright red collar. She was climbing the tree in my front yard. So agile and energetic. Getting about halfway up the tall tree trunk and then leaping off like a wild leopard. I LOVED her instantly.

Opening my front door, I called to her. She immediately looked up at me and ran inside. No reservations, no sense of stranger danger. She was purring, rubbing against my legs. Flopping down on the living room carpet and asking for belly rubs. My God. My favorite type of cat! She ate up attention and was so damn cuddly. I began to wonder, where did she come from? Was she lost? She must be missing from her home. She obviously had owners who cared enough to put that beautiful collar around her neck.

I just couldn't send her back out the door without trying to find her owners and get them reunited. I posted a picture of her on social media asking if anyone was missing her. The replies began flowing in. Questions like, "Does she have a large spot of scar tissue on her left side?" and, "How big is she compared to average house cat size?" I was busy responding to people's inquiries. One woman from my neighborhood even swung by my house to check and see if it was the cat she had lost a couple months earlier. But alas, she was not.

In a whirlwind of petting this soft, sleek, sassy little kitty a few hours I realized she must need to go out for a potty break. I took her back out to the front yard and watched her carefully. Then a dog started aggressively barking from a nearby house. Kitty got spooked and started running down the sidewalk. I called to her. Really wanting her to stay with me until I could have the peace of mind that she was back in her rightful home. But she was obviously stubborn and independent. She just kept galloping along on the concrete until she was out of my sight. My heart ached a little. I missed her sweet presence already.

A week or two later? Surprise, surprise! Miss Pretty Kitty was back for a visit! I was so happy to see her and she was just as friendly as ever. This time I just decided to enjoy the gift of her company and stop worrying about where she lived. She was a healthy, well fed little thing. I was thrilled to get to see her again.

Her visits became pretty regular. Then one night Lefty and I were standing out near our mailbox talking to our next-door neighbors. They were saying something about their dog. It dawned on me that I never even thought to ask them if they had a cat. So I posed the question to the wife. She said yes, they had gotten a cat a while back. I asked what it looked like. She described Miss Pretty Kitty to the T.

Jesus Christ, I thought to myself, *I almost gave away the neighbors' cat!* That was a close one. Glad the sweet little creature had the sense to sprint off down the road the first day we met. A couple more visits by people searching for lost pets and someone may have mistaken her for their own, and I would have had a lot of explaining to do to the nice couple next door.

Update: I haven't seen that sweet kitty in my yard in a long time. I miss her!!! Running into my neighbor the other day, she mentioned that the cat went missing. She was putting up signs around the neighborhood with no luck yet. She was such a friendly little thing that I assume someone found her like I did, only this time they didn't let her go. Probably kept her for their own.

Lefty and I don't have any pets anymore. The guinea pigs moved to Chloë's apartment a while back. So, I got the bright idea to order a bird feeder online. It took forever to arrive, along with the bird seed. But when it did, my oh my! The front yard began to come alive!! Too many different kinds of birds to count flocked to our place for hours on end. I would stare out my kitchen window for ages. Mesmerized by my newfound feathery friends. And then one day even a huge gray squirrel was perched in the tree eating some of the critter food I put out. When I opened the door it looked at me like, "What the hell you looking at?" I promptly closed the door.

The following day? Even more visitors. In addition to about twenty small birds, there was a feisty blue jay, three doves and a woodpecker. I felt so proud. My feeding project had paid off. My heart was happy. The only scary part? Soon after the bird feeder arrived I looked out the window in horror and awe to see an enormous hawk eyeing the little structure. All the other birds had their little bird radar go off and hid in the bushes, but I hoped the hawk wasn't going to make a habit of showing up. A friend reminded me that if it did continue coming around and started eating the little birds, I was still technically "feeding the birds." But that just felt sinister and wrong. Luckily I haven't seen Mr. Hawk again. That's a good thing.

Chapter 99

My Worst Nightmare

Gwen's middle of the night sneaking out fiasco was months ago, and I had finally started to breathe easy(ish). Then one day she told me she started her period two weeks early. I told her sometimes that happens, especially at her age. The age of sixteen is so close to being a full adult, yet the young female body is sometimes still working out a few details so it can run smoothly. But she didn't seem comforted by my reassurance. She seemed like she was working herself into a panic. At first I brushed it off as Gwen being Gwen. She is very good at making mountains out of mole hills. My beautiful little drama queen. But, alas, there was sooooo much more to this story.

She and I were running errands around town and it finally dawned on me to ask if she had been worried she might be pregnant. It was all I could think of when it came to her odd stress over starting to bleed two weeks early. She got real quiet in the passenger seat next to me, and I started feeling incredibly nervous. To my knowledge she hadn't had any recent sexual activity. But I quickly became aware that there were a lot of things I didn't know.

She slowly began to confess that while Lefty and I were away in San Francisco for a football game the weekend prior, she snuck out of the house (AGAIN). I felt so stupid. I was going to make her sleep over at her sister's apartment so I didn't have to worry about her getting into trouble. But at the last minute she called me and said she was just really tired and wanted to sleep in her own bed. All I could think was, *Where the fuck had my mother's intuition gone that night?* and, *Why did it fail me once again?*

Gwen told me, sheepishly, that she met up with a college boy she knew. At his apartment. They drank alcohol and had sex. And oh how I wish I could say that was all. But it so happens he had some shady friend over at the time, too. And after Gwen fell asleep, she was awakened by the guy coming on to her. She tried to tell him no. And the part that breaks my heart even more is that she asked him to drive her home. She told him she was tired and just wanted to sleep. He didn't fucking care, and he proceeded to aggressively rape my daughter. After she expressly told him she was not interested in having sex with him.

When Gwen told me all of this something broke deep down in my soul. All the times I had worked to protect her and keep her safe. All the days I made her take the mace when she walked with her friends, just in case. Those memories washed over me and cruelly pointed out that *I was not there to protect her.* I felt powerless to take her pain away. And I was suddenly gripped by this realization that everything would be different from here on out. She was scarred for life in one of the worst ways possible and there was nothing I could do about it. And had I known it was about to become unbearably worse, I think I would have gone off the deep end. Right then and there.

In the days that followed, Gwen did the responsible thing and made an appointment at Planned Parenthood for STI testing. Her sister offered to take her, and I thought it would be good for them to spend some time together, so I agreed. But a couple hours later, when Gwen came walking through the door with bandages on both arms and a grief stricken look on her face I knew the appointment did not go well. I tried to stay calm as I talked to her in her room. But who was I kidding? I was dying inside and she hadn't even spilled the bad news yet. I guess I already knew.

I kept telling her it would be ok as she cried in despair on her bed. And Gwen kept saying, "No, Mom, it's *not* going to be ok. It's *not!*" My nerves were hanging on by a thread as I kept working to coax the truth out of her. I had to know what was going on. And fast. She finally told me after the tenth time I asked. She had been given a panel of tests, one of which was a quick initial test for HIV. That test came back positive. *IT CAME BACK FUCKING POSITIVE.* It was the most terrified I'd ever been for Gwen. I'd worried about a million things while raising her, but everything in the past paled in comparison. This was not the deal. This was not supposed to be happening. I kept telling her it could be a false positive. She said, "Yes, that's what the clinician told me, too. But what if it's *not*?" I could see the terror in her big blue eyes. My heart sank.

I left Gwen's room a minute to get us both some water, and Lefty asked me what was wrong. He was visibly worried. I told him. About everything. The sneaking out. The rape. The test results. I could barely get the words out while crying so hard, but he understood what I said and was completely horrified. He hugged me hard and said reassuring words about hoping the results were not accurate, but I could feel that he was every bit as scared as I was for our girl.

The days stretching out in front of us were agonizing. Waiting until she could go back in for follow-up testing. We all went up and down with our moods every other moment. One second I was able to find relief that at least I still had Gwen in my life. She was alive and perfectly healthy for the time being. Shouldn't I be thankful? Thankful she was not murdered by the asshole who raped her? She was not thrown away in a college dumpster like trash. Or submerged in a body of water never to be found. But the fear of what this all meant for her life moving forward and the stigma attached to this type of diagnosis was a sharp wound in my emotional orbit. Completely and utterly unbearable.

Her fierce spirit carries her through to brighter days.

Three days after the news, I was driving to pick Gwen up from school and this wave crashed into me. A wave of absolute desperation. And with tears pouring down my face I began to pray. I prayed to God to take away this affliction from my daughter. I begged God to let her test be a false positive. I pleaded and cried while saying it was all I asked. Nothing else. I didn't care in that moment if this book ever got published, didn't care if my music goals ever panned out. Didn't care if I lived the rest of my life broke, always striving for success but never finding it. I just wanted my girl to be alright. *Please let her be alright.*

And guess what? She was. That very same day Gwen got a call from Planned Parenthood confirming that the more extensive blood tests found no sign of HIV. None. It was some of the best news we ever received. And you and I both know I'm not normally a praying woman, but on that day I was elated my prayers were answered. A true miracle for Gwen and for our family. There were still counseling appointments to make and a whole lot of sadness to defuse, but she was alright.

And a month later we took her back for another test just to have total peace of mind. It came back perfect again. She had a second chance at a healthy life. And I had a second chance as a mother. Trying my damnedest to be there for her in any way she needed. It's been a crazy journey and we are all changed because of it. But I think the change is for the better.

Lefty and I ran the case by law enforcement to see if there was a chance at prosecuting the guy who victimized Gwen, but we all came to the same conclusion: Gwen would be dragged through the mud if it went to trial, and the rapist would get off scott free due to no preserved physical evidence. I was afraid it would harm her more to try to hold her own while being cross-examined by defense lawyers. Lawyers who would shame her for not being perfect and take glee in victim-blaming to the fullest.

Gwen knows how lucky she is and seems to be viewing herself with more care. What happened to her was not her fault. She knows she didn't make great decisions that night, but she also knows that she never, ever deserved to be raped. It makes me physically ill to even have to say that word in relation to her. I can't stand it. She is a treasure. Any young man who has the privilege of being in her life down the road is gonna have to be the kindest of the kind. Nothing less. Otherwise I will want to murder him with my bare hands. So done with anyone messing with my girl.

Chapter 100

Do you ever get the feeling that Kayleigh McEnany is really a Donald Trump love child from one of his Barbie mistresses?

There's no chapter to go with this title, I just wanted to throw this question out there for good measure.

Chapter 101

Strong Female Singers: Yes!

Lefty and I were given tickets to a Wynonna Judd concert in our city. They were gifted to my dad by his neighbor then my dad passed them along to us. I was so thankful, because I could not have spent $140 on tickets right now, but a free concert by one of my all time sheroes? Yes please!

We arrived and searched quite a while for a parking space. Finally found one a few blocks away from the historic Cascade Theatre where the concert was taking place. Walking along the sidewalk with Lefty, I had to let him know that my heels were a little too high to walk briskly, so I'd have to cross the street a bit slower than usual. But hey, we were on our way to see Wynonna. One of the greatest divas on earth. I couldn't very well *not* wear fabulous silver strappy Steve Madden heels, right? In fact, they were the ones I originally ordered to wear with my wedding dress, but when they arrived I realized they were gonna be scary to walk in. I didn't want to risk having a Jennifer Lawrence moment as I climbed the stairs to say "I do" to my groom. I Love JLaw, by the way.

The crowd was thick as we waited to enter the theatre. Once we had our ticket barcodes scanned, and our neon green bracelets stating that yes, in fact, we had shown our IDs and were proven to be over the age of twenty-one (needed in order to purchase alcohol), we walked in to find our seats. We were on the aisle in the center orchestra section. L 201 and L 202. Awesome vantage point. There was a smokey haze hanging in the air, probably from a sound check and run through earlier. Apparently the fog machine was working and ready to set the mood.

On the stage I counted twelve to fifteen different instruments waiting to be played by the musical geniuses from Nashville biding their time behind the curtain. A beautiful upright bass, multiple mandolins, several different kinds of guitars and standard basses as well. Along with a steel guitar and one of the most impressive drum sets I've seen in a while.

Not long after standing in line for beer and then settling back into our seats, the announcer came out to get the crowd ready for the show. Billy Pilgrim, from our local country station Q97. I've listened to his and

Patrick John's morning show as long as I can remember. Always fun to see them in person. They are legends around here. Local celebrities who bring us the morning traffic report and entertain us during our reluctant commutes to work.

The band finally arrived on stage, minus Wynonna, to warm up the audience for the woman of the hour. They were great. High energy, unique sound, and each one a character in and of himself. During an intermission later in the night I looked up the band members and found that the drummer was actually Wynonna's husband, Cactus Moser. Yes, Cactus. It just *don't get no more country than that y'all!* In addition to being a phenomenal drummer, he was an amazing singer, too. I was impressed.

About forty minutes into the show, the moment we'd all been waiting for was upon us, a stunning, sparkly (literally, she was covered in glitter and rhinestones from head to toe) redhead stepped onto the stage and the voice that came from her body was almost otherworldly. "Clouds in the sky...you know how I feel. Birds flyin' high...you know how I feel..." She definitely started the show off on a "feel good" note. And it just kept going from there. Wynonna Judd's voice is one of the iconic voices in America that evokes so much power it's simply surreal to see her in person. Jaw-dropping and unforgettable.

Towards the end of the evening, she said something that made an impact. She said, "I thank God for blessing me with such a long, fulfilling career. I think he knew I would have never made it at a real job." Then she laughed. I laughed, too. Then I started to cry. Bittersweet tears welled up in my eyes and my heart started hurting. But it was a good hurt. A hurt telling me there are others out there like me. People like Wynonna who have followed their passion fully, and had so much to show for it. It made me feel less crazy for struggling in every mainstream position I've ever had. Less crazy for knowing why I was born, and what I wanted out of life. My wants and desires and passions are not too much to ask for or aspire to. They're not. I thank people like Wynonna for setting an incredible example of female talent, strength, tenacity, and paving the way for all of us who dream of following in her footsteps. "No One Else On Earth" can do it like she does. But we can try, damn it. We can try.

Update: Another concert hot on the heels of the one above. For my daughter Chloë's birthday this year, her Grandma Rain was kind enough to buy her a ticket to a concert of her choice, and buy an extra one for whichever guest she chose to take with her. So...the concert she chose? Pink! The guest she chose? Me!!! One lucky mother right here!

The show was in Sacramento, only about two and a half hours from our place here in Redding. But I'm such a country bumpkin that I was a little nervous about navigating the trip without my husband, so I asked my mom and younger daughter to come along with us. Girls trip! Upon first setting out, *my girls* were fighting like cats in the back seat. Chloë and Gwen apparently hadn't traveled together for a while and had a whole lot of shit to get off their chest in a very rude and incessant fashion. Lord help us…

As the day wore on things mellowed for a little while, but when we arrived at the hotel in Sac where I reserved a room the day before, it looked like a place where we would *definitely* get murdered in our sleep. And even the fact that a police department was across the street didn't make me feel any safer. So we canceled my reservation over the phone. It took us three tries for the nice guy on the other end of the line to allow us to do so, but we did succeed. Then we hovered in a Costco parking lot frantically Googling another place to stay that wasn't $400 a night and didn't have a neon sign out front saying "No Vacancy."

Finally we spotted something promising. The girls called to enquire, then handed me the phone to seal the deal. When we got there it looked surprisingly "un-rapey." Thank goodness. I felt good about Mom and Gwen hanging out there while Chloë and I went to the concert a couple miles away.

Long story short, the show was mind-blowingly amazing. Pink is the real fucking deal. I've always known it, but seeing her live was insane. I really don't have the adequate words to describe it. Just go see her for yourself. You will not be dissapointed!!!

Chapter 102

The End Is Our Beginning

My husband and I watched the last episode of "The Americans" tonight. My eyes were wet the whole time, even amidst all the suspense. The show came to us via a streaming service, so we saw it long after it had already wrapped up on actual television. In case you're contemplating checking out what all the fuss was about, I won't spoil the ending for you. What I will say is that it made me think long and hard about why we come into this world, what we are here to do, and the unavoidable fact that everything must come to an end.

The spies in the show came to America in order to protect their country. They came with good intentions, but in the process they did a lot of bad things to good people.

There are stretches in life when we play the villain in someone else's movie. There are also times when we play the hero in their favorite show. Sometimes we play both in the same instance. Things exist that we've all done that have imprinted on certain individuals' minds in such a way that they will never forget nor forgive us. And if we're lucky, there are things we've done that have affected others in such a positive way they would speak up for us in a crowded room full of judgemental detractors.

When it comes down to it, all we can do is keep perfecting ourselves under ever-growing pressure to pretend we are somebody else. We owe it to the world to be us. I truly believe the journey of self-discovery is at least ninety percent of the reason we were born. Because when we find ourselves, our true selves, we help others do the same. We set an example that says to those around us, "Hey, you can do this, too. I believe in you. You are *allowed* to believe in yourself."

There is no shortage of uphill battles while we are inhabiting human bodies and human minds. But our challenges are our teachers. We can handle the climb. And when we reach the top, the view will be beautiful. I promise.

Chapter 103

Being American

I suffer from a strong sense of shame over being American. Especially a white American. This feeling of needing to apologize for a whole lot of atrocities my ancestors committed. My great, great, great grandfather fought in the Civil War. He was a Union soldier, thank God. And he gave his life far too young during that bloodbath of a conflict. So I suppose I don't have to be ashamed of *all* my ancestry, just some. The Civil War aspect along with my Polish Jew heritage makes me proud. My great grandfather from Mississippi, however? Not so much. But we're not going to talk about him here.

I had a blissful moment the other day during a work training exercise. The speaker asked us to share one word we just really hated. Someone said, "Bitch." Another said, in a quiet voice, "The C word." Then the sweet older lady to my left said, "Trump." I laughed and replied, "Right on! Me, too!" The woman to *her* right did not appear to be amused.

Chapter 104

Memories

I tend to have a rather unusual memory. Specifics of conversations often elude me, which gets me into hot water with my daughters. They'll say things like, "Mom! You said we could go!" or "Mommy!! You told me you would take me today!" and here I am thinking to myself, "Did I really say that?"

Sometimes I won't remember a single detail about conversations I've been a party to. And no, I'm not just talking about the mornings after a group function with too much Hennessy being passed around. It's like I have selective amnesia. Is it just because a conversation doesn't spark my interest, or because it stresses me out, that I don't file it away in its own compartment in my brain? I don't know. But what I find fascinating are the things I *do remember.* Often random things that appear to have no real relevance to what was taking place at the time, yet here they are, seared into my mind's eye for all eternity.

Like the time I got super sick as a child when I was sleeping over at a friend's house. I was wearing a white turtleneck with tiny red hearts splashed all over the surface. I remember the brown leather sandals I took to Paris with me. The ones that, for some bizarre reason, stained the bottom of my feet a god awful orange. Kind of like the hue of Donald Trump's skin.

I remember being embroiled in a heated argument shortly before my divorce from my ex-husband. I told him I didn't realize I had signed up for such a struggle when we got together. I didn't know I would have to compete so much, and always lose, for his attention amongst all his ups and downs and addictions to everything under the sun. In return, he told me that he didn't think he signed up for being married to a fat American. I was a size six at the time. I stood there trying to figure out whether he meant what he said, or whether he was just lashing out because he was mad at me for calling him on his shit. I was wearing a turquoise-colored sweatshirt.

The first time Lefty kissed me we were on our first date, walking down the sidewalk in the dark. Heading to a bar close by. Street lights shining down in splotchy patterns on the two of us, he stopped abruptly, turned towards me and took my face in his hands. Touched his lips to mine as if I was already his. No hesitation. I felt so safe and wanted. In all the right ways. I distinctly remember the magic that hung thick in the air that night. I still feel it when I'm with him. It never went away.

Memories wash over us at the strangest moments in time. Sometimes they're like recurring dreams, and for the life of us we can't figure out why they are branded so boldly in our minds. Why do I recall the first time my elementary school boyfriend held my hand, but it's a blank slate when I try to conjure up the first time my ex-husband said I love you? I can see what I was wearing right down to the shoes on my feet in every job interview I've ever had, but I don't remember what I wore for my first day as a new hire for any of my positions.

We can't really choose our memories, can we? There are so many of mine that I would love to wish away into the graveyard of life experiences I didn't want to have. But like a loyal dog, they keep showing up by my side, with a smile on their face, wagging their tail, asking for a treat.

They say eyewitness testimonies in crime cases are fatally flawed. The getaway car was green, but someone swears it was brown. There were only three assailants, when in actuality there were more than five. The human imagination is so active and can be suggestive to the point that we fill in blanks that never existed in the first place. We are capable of tailoring our recollections to fit our narratives, and most of the time we don't even know we're doing it. I've been mistaken enough times about what color an object was, or how old I was when a given trauma happened, that I have learned to second guess my stories I tell myself. Leave room for operator error. Especially if it's on an important topic.

Do you ever wish we could each have a secret video of our lives? One where we can fast forward and rewind in order to remedy untruths we have taken as fact for too long? Or would that option induce a special type of insanity we don't need in our existence? Are some things meant to be misremembered? Morphed into something kinder? Perhaps shaving down the pain until it's tolerable to the touch?

Chapter 105

A Sudden Shock

Lefty got some terrible news yesterday. One of his best friends died. No one saw it coming. There was no warning. He just woke up in the night and couldn't breathe. His parents tried to save him and also called paramedics, but to no avail. His sweet friend was gone and no one got to say goodbye. In Lao culture, friends and family of a loved one who has passed gather for many nights in a row at the loved one's house. They bring food, drinks, hugs. It's part of the tradition of supporting and comforting those who are hurting so much from loss. I'm sure there's more to the meaning of these gatherings I have yet to understand, but this is what I observe when we participate.

I went with my husband last night to his friend's family home. I used to not understand how people could want company when they were in so much pain, but I've come to realize it's the company that allows them to ease into the darkness of grief, rather than plunge in head first all at once. These gatherings are an incredible display of devotion in Lefty's community. The bonds are strong. The love runs deep. My heart breaks for my husband. He has lost a shocking number of people close to him over the years. He lost his father when he was fifteen.

When Lefty and I first started dating, we realized that we had something in common. We had both lost a loved one in our immediate family. It was the first time I didn't have to describe to the man I was with how grief felt. And why I was so messed up by it. He knew exactly how it felt, how it never stops, how it stays with us for life. I'm a little ashamed to admit how comforting that was for me. I felt less alone. But I obviously wish to God that my husband never had to endure such anguish. I would have been okay with explaining my pain if it meant that he never had to experience it first hand at such a young age.

In the next week or so we will go to the memorial for his friend. We will lay to rest another piece of Lefty's big heart, and It's already breaking mine to think about. I will try to be strong for him, but we both know I will fail, and I will cry more than he does. I've never seen a tear drop from his eyes. Only well up with a bit of wetness. He deserves a vacation from the ever-present reminders of mortality. I know that's unrealistic, but if I could give that to him, I would.

Chapter 106

Fire

I just finished watching a country music awards show. Everyone was crowded into the middle of downtown Nashville. Beloved Broadway Street with all the neon bar signs shining bright. Bars where I've enjoyed countless shots of whiskey, been so proud to see my brother perform, even sung a couple tunes myself over the years. While watching this beautiful display of artists doing what they do best, a strong feeling welled up inside me. I can only describe it as a yearning, a burning in my soul. No, not like the devil trying to get me. I don't believe in the devil anyway. I'd like to see him try. But a burning which started as a smolder of embers and in five more seconds became a full on bonfire raging towards the dark sky.

I still want that music career I've always dreamt of. I want to perform on those multilevel stages. I try hard not to want this, because I worry it will take a toll on my family, but there's gotta be a way to do it all. I know Lefty will be a great travel partner for book tours and music tours alike. He's the husband I was always meant to find. He'll journey with me. And I say, "Let's *go for it!!!*" It's time to learn to stop holding myself back. Time to allow myself to accept my "wants" as practical plans to strive for. It is *not too much* to ask for everything under the sun. With free twenty-four hour shipping and a sprinkling of fairy dust included in the box.

Chapter 107

I'm Still That Girl

"When a flower doesn't bloom, you fix the environment in which it grows, not the flower."
– Alexander Den Heijer

I quit my job today. There were no drop the mic moments like I fantasized about for so long. Just an honest talk with my boss, a resignation letter, and an overwhelming feeling of pure joy which could not be contained. I'm done dying a little bit every day. I mean, as humans, isn't that what we're doing already? Why the hell would we want to accelerate the process? I'm ready to live. I'm ready to write. I'm ready to songwrite, sing, and paint. I'm even ready to dance, and I *can't* dance. I'm ready to be me. Because after all...This is who I *really* am.

When my life flashes before my eyes I see years upon years of struggling toward the light. Trying to accept the qualities about myself I don't understand. I've worked too many times to mold myself into someone else's ideal shape. But I'm done with cookie cutters that shear away some of my favorite parts of me. I'm done walking through life feeling less than competent and misunderstood by others. I'm done tormenting my psyche by making myself stick to a plan completely inappropriate for my well being. I keep telling myself I deserve to be happy. And for the first time in my entire life, *I believe this to be true.*

Deep down I'm still the girl I always was. Full of dreams and goals that conventional society views as unrealistic. But I know in my heart they're real. I was, am, and always will be that girl who doesn't take no for an answer when barriers stand in my way. The one who's afraid of death, but trying her hardest not to be afraid of life. I am *still* that girl with sand in her hair, who is unashamed to be standing naked in the river.

Photo: Jil Chipman

Acknowledgments

Thank you, **Helen M. Stone** for doing the first edit of *Naked in the River* for me! You are an amazing woman and I am honored to call you my friend. I wish you ridiculously good things in your life. Only good is what you deserve. And puppies. Lots of puppies!

***

I want to thank my husband, **Leutvilay (Lefty) Khamsaly.** You walked into my life with your charming smile and GQ good looks at a time when I had almost stopped believing in love, and showed me a type of devotion I could not have imagined in my own mind's creation. The depth of your soul is boundless and the depth of my love for you is without description. It is bigger than any words can articulate.

The other night I wrote a love letter to you, but never left it on your nightstand, so here it is:

> *I am continually surprised that you love me. All I've ever known of romantic love is that it ends. But you continue to love me, and I continue to love you. And it is a love that whispers of the ages. Of days gone by and all the sunrises to come. You and I must have met before. Because our love is such that cannot merely be cultivated over the course of a handful of years. It takes lifetime upon lifetime to grow this powerful. I look forward to spending the rest of my lifetimes with you. Keeper of my heart, healer of my soul. Lefty, you light the flame that illuminates the brightest part of me, and I am divinely grateful.*

***

To my daughters:

Chloë, you made me a mother when it was the furthest thing from my plans. You transformed my life and opened my eyes to what it feels like to love a tiny being more than I love myself. What you have given to me I can never repay, but I will spend the rest of my life trying. You are strong and incredibly beautiful, kind and wise. Deeply compassionate. Adorably meticulous with homework projects and picking out pets and tattoos. I am in awe of you and I love you endlessly, all the way to the moon and back!

Gwen, you are mesmerizing. Such a deep soul and wonderfully intense human being. You were an incredibly joyful surprise when you decided to enter this world. Stunning and hilarious beyond belief, you make me angry as hell, happy beyond words, and when I'm around you, I laugh like crazy. You have such passion for life. Strong feminist wisdom beyond your years, just like your sister. Never a dull moment spent with my sweet Gwen. I love you completely, always and forever!

***

To my step-sons:

Cameron, thank you for welcoming me into your life years ago when your father and I met. I'm sure it wasn't easy, but I loved you from the beginning, and I love you now. You are bright eyed and intelligent, growing up so handsome. I very much enjoy seeing you become taller by the second! I look forward to watching your life path. You will do wonderful things!

Jarron, what a dignified, powerful young man you are! So good looking like your father. Brave as a lion, kind as the warmth of the sun. Thank you for blessing us with your presence. I sincerely hope it is just the start of being lucky enough to get to know who you are and what your hopes and dreams hold for you in this life!

***

A special shout out to **Jim Hyatt**, one of my music producers and dearest friends:

You have always been a sounding board for my creative endeavors. And when I get around to that random phone call every six months, I can count on you to pick me up out of a bad mood at the drop of a hat.

Jim, your feedback is worth more than gold, and I wish you all the best all the time!

***

I thank my father, **Randall**, for instilling my love of music, and for teaching me so much about it as a young child. And for setting an example as an activist for what is right and standing up for those who cannot stand up for themselves.

***

My sister, **Naomi**, for teaching me that life is short, and adventures are a must. And for blessing me with your striking and powerful presence during your all too brief life. You taught me to be strong. I had no choice but to find my strength when you left. The love I carry in my heart for you is an overgrown flower garden. Wild and blowing in the breeze. Smelling softly of purple lilac and keeping all its honeybees in a state of eternal bliss.

***

And my dear brother, **Sid**, for a million reasons. Making me laugh at your stupid jokes, even when they're at my expense. For co-producing my Nashville album years ago and lending your beautiful fiddle playing to it. For being one of my very best friends and the most wonderful uncle to Chloë and Gwen. And for helping shape who I am and who I have always tried to become in order to make you and the rest of our family proud.

***

And to my mother, **Nicola**, who has supported me in too many ways to count. You are my rock, my hero, my example beyond all other examples. I could not be doing what I am doing today without having had the boundless, unconditional love and kindness you have shown me every second of every day since giving birth to me. You are an example for all of humanity on how to live one's life while doing no harm, sharing your truth, and striving for a peaceful and compassionate existence.

Thank you endlessly for never giving up on me, Mom. All my years of crazy endeavors and big plans. The energy you poured into me has paid off in these pages. We did this together. You are the most beautiful person on earth!

***

Last but not least, thank you, **Ginna and David Gordon** of Lucky Valley Press! Your amazing guidance and editing is a godsend. What a joy to work with you both! Thanks for being patient with my quirky writing style and unorthodox approach. I'm so honored that you were willing to take my project on and make it shine!

About the Author

Arianna Vivian Khamsaly is an American Singer-Songwriter, Nashville Recording Artist, and Author. Also a Head-in-the-Clouds-Dreamer, Devoted Mother, Lucky Wife, and Unapologetic Feminist. A strong Believer in Human Rights and Racial Justice, she was born in a log cabin on the outskirts of a tiny town in far Northern California.

Raised skinny dipping in the rivers, running barefoot on her childhood property, and learning to think outside the box, Arianna was home-schooled most of her upbringing, and had to get creative in ways to entertain herself.

She turned to writing, singing, songwriting, and visual arts as a means of self expression and as an escape from often crushing loneliness in the midst of life in such a remote location.

Music and art run in Arianna's family. Her father is a renowned music teacher, singer and musician, her brother is a professional fiddle player who spent twenty years playing for stars out of Nashville, and her mother is a UC Berkeley Art Major.

Arianna resides with her husband, Lefty, and their kids in Redding, California, while traveling to Nashville periodically to enjoy being immersed in the soul of Music City.

Her most recent music release is an EP called *Anywhere But Here*, four original tracks that speak of love, loss, individuality and the confines of conventionality in America today.

Contact Arianna through her website:

www.ariannaviviankhamsaly.com

Download and Stream Arianna's New Music Now!

For downloads, streaming, and social media:
linktr.ee/ariannavkhamsaly

www.ingramcontent.com/pod-product-compliance
Lightning Source LLC
LaVergne TN
LVHW010054170826
845678LV00012B/2139

* 9 7 8 0 5 7 8 3 3 7 2 6 5 *